D0494790

BATH S DISCARD

The Voiceover Handbook

Practical advice for aspiring and established voiceover artists

Gary Churcher

Paul Bridge

Voiceovers Ltd. Publishing

B.S.U.C. - LIBRARY

00336496

The Voiceover Handbook, First Edition

Published by Voiceovers Ltd. Publishing
PO Box 326, Plymouth, PL4 9YQ
Copyright © Voiceovers Ltd. Publishing 2010

All rights reserved. No parts of this publication may be reproduced, stored in a retrieval system or transmitted, in any form or by any means, electronic, mechanical, photocopying, recording, scanning or otherwise, now known or hereafter invented, without the prior permission of the publishers. All trademarks are the property of their respective owners.

Warning and Disclaimer

The information contained in this book is distributed on an "as is" basis, without warranty. Every precaution has been taken to make this book as complete and as accurate as possible and neither the authors nor Voiceovers Ltd. shall have any liability or responsibility to any person or entity with respect to any loss or damages arising directly or indirectly from information contained within this book. The authors and Voiceovers Ltd. are NOT RESPONSIBLE whatsoever for any injury that may result from practising techniques given within. Always consult a physician prior to attempting any new exercise. The advice contained in this work may not be suitable for every situation and the fact that a website or organisation may be referred to does not mean that the authors or Voiceovers Ltd. endorse information gained via the website or organisation or any recommendations it makes. Please always refer to your lawyer before creating, adapting or using any legal documents (for example a licensing agreement or your standard terms and conditions) to ensure they are fit for purpose.

A catalogue record of this book is available from the British Library.

10 9 8 7 6 5 4 3 2

ISBN 978-0-9567438-0-0

Printed in the UK by Copytech (UK) Ltd.

BATH SPA UNIVERSITY
NEWTON PARK LIBRARY
Class No.
791.4028 CHu
30)11)20

DISPLAY

Our story started in 1997 when we had an idea to launch the first online, searchable website to promote voice artists. At a time before broadband, Google, MP3 players and the BBC News website, it was pretty radical! We realised that the voiceover industry had already started changing and that the internet would play an important role. A year later in 1998 we launched Voiceovers.co.uk.

Now we're about 12 years on and at our strongest yet. Our website has gone through redesigns and revamps but we still have the same aim: to get our voiceover artists lots of work!

It's become even more fun for us. We now promote more than 400 voice artists, arrange recordings for corporate clients, perform casting for big brands and work in many different languages and studios across the world. There's nothing more satisfying than hearing one of our voices on a high profile TV advert, or having one of our recordings used on a successful viral campaign or product launch.

We've learned from every demo we've listened to, recording session that we've arranged and artist we've advised, and we decided to create this book. We've tried to answer the most common questions that you would ask, and also some of those you didn't know you should be asking. We've tried to cover all areas most relevant to the voiceover industry today, from home studios to marketing.

Some of what you'll read is common sense to the professional, but not always common practice. The newbies should gain some fundamental knowledge, the old timers learn new tricks, and those inbetween, check they are doing everything to maximise their success.

If you're thinking about getting into the industry then it should give you a good insight as to what is required. If you decide the industry is not right for you, then at least you have done your research and made an informed decision before spending too much time or money.

The book is laid out as a series of questions, grouped into chapters for each aspect of the industry.

You might want to simply refer to specific questions as they crop up; however to get the most out of the book we do recommend you read all the questions and visit our associated website www.voiceoverhandbook.co.uk.

Introduction (p1)

Contents

Contents

Chapter 10: Improving Your Voice Quality (p155)

Chapter 11: Voiceover Rates (p171)

Chapter 12: The Future of Voiceovers (p187)

Contents

Chapter 13: Tips to Make You Stand Out (p191)

13.1 What tips can you give to make me better than the competition?

Appendix A (p195)

Sample Terms and Conditions

Appendix B (p199)

Sample Licence Agreement

Appendix C (p203)

Sample Scripts

Appendix D (p209)

Sample Invoice

Glossary (p211)

In the last 30 years the UK voiceover industry has adapted to the effects of global connectivity, the internet revolution, decreasing technology prices and increased media channels. The traditional London voice agency business model has been challenged, and at the same time opportunities have grown for independent voiceover artists based throughout the UK. These voiceovers have flourished, by installing their own professional home studios offering comparable quality to London studios, and have been well placed to serve the growing demand caused by the explosion of digital media and the internet.

With increased voice choice and competition, this has affected the way voiceover artists need to position and market themselves. In the past a voice artist's skill rested solely with their voice; the artists who succeeded were those who were very versatile and able to perform a host of accents and styles with ease. The most gifted would usually relocate to London and an agent would promote them. These artists did not need to worry about technical issues or how to market themselves; they concentrated on their voice skills.

Producers have made the most of the additional voice options and there has been a trend towards "realism", using a larger pool of voices from the full spectrum of accents and ages. Voiceover use is all about communication: "getting the message across" in an effective and appropriate way. Thus behind the scenes it is recognised that the best voice for each project can be affected by marketing, brand establishment, sociology and psychology. More than ever, being a voiceover artist is less about being versatile and a jack of all trades, and more about being yourself and defining what you do best. Successful voice artists now tend to be those who position themselves as leading in a specific area, style or accent. They have enough technical know-how to make their own professional recordings, and can do this quickly and efficiently.

We think this is a truly exciting time to be involved in the voiceover industry, and that the voiceover artists who continue to succeed will be those who are increasingly aware of what is expected of them, and who keep one step ahead of the game.

Chapter 1

Initial Questions Aspiring Voices Ask

1.1   What action plan would you suggest?

- Find out what is required of you, skim read this book.

- Perform market analysis to gauge whether there is enough demand for your style of voice (Question 1.2).

- Practise with your voice intensively for a few months and discover your own limitations; consider voice coaching (Chapter 7: Script Preparation; Chapter 8: Voice Delivery and Technique; Chapter 10: Improving Your Voice Quality).

- Critically evaluate your own vocal abilities and decide whether a career as a voiceover is right for you (Question 1.3).

- Look at your recording studio options and set up your own studio if this forms part of your business model (Chapter 5: Equipment and Studio Sound).

- If you have your own studio, teach yourself how to record and deliver your own recordings (Chapter 6: Recording Yourself – Technical Considerations).

- Prepare your demo audio (Chapter 4: Demos) and get feedback to refine it before launching.

- Get your business affairs in order (Chapter 2: Basic Business).

- Establish your brand, set up your own website and consider getting an agent (Chapter 3: Branding and Marketing).

- Decide how you are going to set your rates and cost up jobs (Chapter 11: Voiceover Rates).

- Market yourself. Consider a "soft launch" and reinforce demo audio before launching on a larger scale. (Chapter 3: Branding and Marketing).

- When you're up and running, look at how you can get an edge over your competitors (Chapter 13: Tips to Make You Stand Out) and continually try to improve and update your demo audio.

1.2   Is there a demand for my voice?

In the business world, however good a product is, there has to be enough demand to make it into a viable business, and the voiceover industry is no different. You won't be able to gauge whether there is a demand for your voice until you undertake some market research.

We think a useful exercise is to search for professional voiceover artists who have the same style, age and tone (and native accent perhaps) as you. If you cannot find people that you would be competing with, because you have a unique ability, then this can be an encouraging sign. As a good starting place, have a look on www.voiceovers.co.uk.

Of the voices that you consider equivalent to you, in what ways could you effectively compete against them? Do they have their own studio? Are they available at short notice? How much experience do they have?

We receive a lot of demos from 30-something voices who have neutral accents and have been told that they have a good voice. Unfortunately this area of the industry is very saturated and positioning yourself in this market is very difficult – especially for a newcomer.

Established voices should constantly monitor demand and their competitors so that they can reposition themselves if required and always stay one step ahead.

1.3   How do I know whether I'm good or not?

If you're a complete beginner, why not try recording yourself at home before you decide to commit additional time and money?

You need to check that you're comfortable with the basics, like reading aloud smoothly. You can test yourself using a microphone connected to your computer or with a cheap dictaphone, mobile phone etc. Find a few pieces of text to read such as narrative, literature or newspaper articles, record yourself and listen back.

You should listen out for problem sounds in certain words that you find difficult to pronounce, consistent volume throughout and how your voice sounds in general. Are you sounding monotonous? Do you sound natural? Compare yourself to other talents by listening to their voice demos.

You can also practise your microphone technique. Are you keeping a consistent distance from the microphone when practising?

Don't be put off if you find the text in books or newspapers too small to follow easily. You can always find some articles online then change the font size and line spacing before you print them.

This exercise is also important so that you familiarise yourself with your own voice. Most people initially think they sound totally different to how they hear themselves in their head. Be aware of how your voice sounds on a good day, so you can spot when you're off the boil.

1.4 Is it worth having my own professional studio?

Having your own studio will give you an advantage, but there are certain costs involved and thousands of pounds of investment is normally required. Running costs such as electricity, telephone etc. can be fairly low in comparison, so the initial setup would be seen as an investment. Whether you should invest in your own professional studio depends on a number of factors. If you are getting regular work in the industry it would be seen as a very good idea, if not essential. It is certainly the way the industry is moving and would give you much more flexibility. You can provide re-records without having to worry about your clients incurring extra studio fees. You must be technically savvy, however, and be able to use a computer, record yourself and have basic editing and internet skills. You may also want to consider setting up a shared studio to save on initial costs.

If you are starting out and have a limited budget, you may wish to invest in a budget studio setup. This would allow you to record yourself to develop your skills, and make your own custom demo samples for auditioning. However you will lose your reputation quickly if you try to operate as a voiceover using a mediocre setup. It's like hiring a plumber who turns up without the proper tools – you'd be disappointed, and probably not book him again. So it's therefore important to be upfront about your studio limitations. If you record your auditions in a non-professional studio, why not suggest a viable professional alternative for the main recording?

Please see Chapter 2, Questions:
2.1 "How much will it cost to start up as a voiceover?"
2.9 "Can I set up my studio on a budget?".

1.5   Is it essential to be based within commuting distance of London?

No, it's not essential, although living in close proximity to central London can have big benefits. Many companies are currently unaware of the different recording methods available, such as listening in using ISDN. This means that much of the lucrative voiceover work will be recorded in a London voiceover studio, with clients directing the session in-person. It's fair to say the industry is adapting to newer technologies and opportunities are opening up to regional voices, but there's a long way to go.

Because the lucrative work is still mostly in the capital and voices may be required at short notice for in-person sessions or auditions, the London agencies' rosters of talent will almost exclusively be London based voiceovers.

London is the main media hub of the UK and so is naturally ideal for networking opportunities.

There are, however, many established voices who are not based near to London and who will be operating from their own professional studios. These voices will utilise ISDN and phone patch and have very good availability to negate any of the issues of not being based in London. For example a voiceover with a home studio can audition for a job immediately with a custom sample and have an advantage over a London based voiceover who has no immediate studio access.

The clever voices will benefit from the best of both worlds by being based within commuting distance of London but also having their own professional studio at home.

1.6 What is the correct term for a voiceover artist?

There are many terms to describe voiceover artists and these are mostly used interchangeably; for example announcer, narrator, voiceover, voice over, voiceover artist, voice artist, voice actor, voice talent.

Some of these terms (such as voice actor) are aimed at a specific area in the industry, so if you're describing yourself just choose a term you feel comfortable with.

1.7   Is there a voiceover community and how do I get accepted?

In the UK there is a vibrant voiceover community. In fact, being a small industry, it has a very friendly atmosphere and many voiceovers will cross paths whilst working on projects. Much of the community is virtual with online forums, because voiceovers are spread right across the UK. Voiceovers get together to discuss common issues such as rates and problem clients, but also to chat about marketing tips and technology. For example, there is a group called "CyberVoices" in the UK which would be worth checking out; this group is solely for established voiceover artists and anything said within the forum is treated in total confidence (www.cybervoices.info).

There is also an annual conference called "Vox" where producers (mainly from the commercial radio scene) and voiceovers will get together to network over a weekend.

Within each geographical region some voiceovers will socialise, either because they're based at the same studio, or simply to help each other out; for example if they're having studio issues. London, as the capital, has its own voiceover scene which revolves mainly around the agency voices who are often in Soho for work.

Because most voiceovers are distinct, there's not as much rivalry as in other industries. Nevertheless, it's a common concern amongst professional voiceovers that if the number of voiceovers grows further, then it will dilute the amount of work available. As such, new voices are often treated with a little suspicion and there will be a period of time when as a "newbie" you'll have to prove yourself and demonstrate that you're bringing something new to the industry.

1.8   Can I be a part-time voiceover?

Unless you're in high demand, being available at very short notice during the working day is a crucial part of being a voiceover. If you attempt to do it on a part-time basis, then you're likely to irritate a lot of producers if you tell them you can't record at a time they suggest. The same goes if they have recorded with you and you're not around to do an urgent pickup. You're unlikely to get a call for return work from these people.

There are a few exceptions: 1) You're a part-time voice but your other job is based in a studio and you have the flexibility to do the odd session within work time; 2) You're a London based agency voice and have a flexible diary that allows you to be booked for sessions with a couple of days notice; 3) You're a part-time voiceover and a part-time mum with a home studio. There are a number of great voiceovers who also take care of their children during the day and juggle the two successfully.

Another consideration is your return on investment. To provide quality recordings will require a quality studio which costs money! This is money you'll have to recoup through voice work and that will take a long time if you're only working part-time. Other ongoing overheads such as ISDN rental will make it an expensive part-time "hobby" rather than a business venture.

1.9   Do I need to join Equity?

To start with, who are they? The Equity website explains:

"Equity is the UK Trade Union representing professional performers and other creative workers from across the spectrum of the entertainment, creative and cultural industries."

Equity membership has many benefits for a voiceover. You'll find that many voices who record local radio commercials will base their fees on "Equity rates". These voices follow the Equity guide of the minimum rate to charge each station for a radio script. Being a member of Equity will allow you access to this rate card.

They can advise on rates for other areas of the market too and are available on telephone/email for these everyday queries.

Membership includes public liability insurance and they can help by chasing money too. They'll initiate and follow through a full small claims procedure on your behalf if necessary.

For a voiceover earning £20-£35k per year, annual membership is approx £200. The fees reflect your volume of work so will vary depending on your income. For the latest rates and more info on benefits just search "Equity benefits" online.

It's not essential to be a member of Equity to be successful in the voiceover industry, but some voices find it reassuring to have their support.

You can visit Equity online at www.equity.org.uk.

1.10   How much can I earn?

The voiceover industry is comparable to other artistic trades such as a freelance artist. They may only do a few paintings a year, and their work is less in demand. Other artists may make hundreds of thousands because their paintings are high profile, popular and the artist markets him/herself well. At a recent voiceover conference, more than 75% of voiceovers who we surveyed were earning a full-time income (more than £15,000 per year).

As a voice artist, we think you shouldn't just consider income; other considerations are quality of life and cost of living. From this perspective, many voice artists find they can work from home, eliminating any travel time and costs, and can fit home life around their day job.

This sounds like an easy life – but bear in mind your effort and availability will reward you. It is possible to make a substantial income in this industry, given your dedication, discipline and marketing. Within the local radio market, we work with some voiceovers who might get three radio scripts a week and others who often receive around 15 a day.

Most voiceovers do not launch and suddenly have a great income; you will find it is a gradual process to establish yourself and build a client base which leads to a more regular income. Don't expect to launch and get lucrative TV work from the outset; it just won't happen. Some voices will start out by subsidising their lifestyle with a second job; others will sacrifice luxuries – either way it takes time to gradually reach a full-time salary.

For specific rates for the different market areas please refer to Chapter 11: Voiceover Rates.

1.11   What if I'm not computer literate?

It's absolutely essential to be computer literate in almost every industry and most certainly for any small business.

You must at least be comfortable with reformatting word documents, emailing, basic sound recording and editing, accessing information from the internet, printing etc.

It would also be beneficial for you to be able to operate an accounts program, keep an electronic diary, and know the basics of FTP programs to allow you to deliver large recordings.

There are many courses that are available to help you if you are not computer literate – so there is no excuse!

For more information try searching online for these terms:
   learning information technology
   computer literacy courses

1.12 What do I need to know about local radio recordings?

The local radio industry doesn't generally pay a high per-script rate but is a worthwhile income for many voiceover artists due to the frequency of bookings. Before marketing yourself for local radio, ensure that you understand the rate structure and be aware that local radio producers usually have tight deadlines and so will often require last minute availability, usually within a couple of hours.

In the UK, ISDN is generally used to record voiceovers for local radio so that the producer can direct and record the session remotely which will generally take less than 15 minutes per script. It is therefore essential to have ISDN if you want to work in this market place.

1.13   Where could my voice be used?

Take a pad and spend a day or even a week making notes when and where you hear professional voices. This may be when you're on the phone, watching TV, in your car, at the supermarket, at the cinema and so on.

How do the voices differ in style and tone? Are they informative? Hard sell? Understanding? Warm? Young? Old? Does the style of voice fit with the brand of the product, company or service?

Sometimes the voices you hear will not be professional – it would be good for you to note what made you realise they were not professional, and whether a professional voice would have made a positive difference.

This is a useful exercise as it demonstrates that a voiceover is not just for radio and TV commercials. You'll probably conclude that your voice could be used everywhere.

1.14   Do I need to get rid of my regional accent?

The short answer is no. A native accent can often be your unique selling point. Gone are the days when voice artists had to speak with a neutral or RP (Received Pronunciation) voice.

It would be useful, however, if you could vary the intensity of your accent, softening or hardening it on demand, and switch to a more neutral voice if required. More than likely you will want to promote your accented natural voice as your primary voice, and anything else as secondary.

We urge you to be yourself – don't try to copy other voices or try to make yourself sound like the "typical voiceover". When you voice a script it's not about you being someone else, it's about you being in a particular situation/mood/time. It's great for your recordings to have a hint of your personality.

It's worth noting that this trend is not just about accents. The fact is there's not a "standard voice" any more. There is less "right" or "wrong" in the industry with style or how you should approach a script. Be yourself and develop your individual style. Obviously you can widen your range and provide what is requested, but you should have a set of default voices and styles which define what your voice is all about.

1.15 I sound exactly like a celebrity. Does this mean I'm quids in?

There are two different routes to this. The first is someone who has a "flexible" voice and can perform convincing character and celebrity impersonations. This is a great skill and can be valuable in the right areas such as cartoons and commercial characters on radio/television ads.

The other is when you naturally sound like a celebrity in your/their normal speaking voice. This doesn't unfortunately mean that you're quids in as you must ask yourself, "Why would the client choose me over a celebrity?" Do you remember the TV show *Stars in Their Eyes*? The Chris de Burgh impersonator was brilliant, really convincing, but when it comes to buying tickets the fans will pay to see the genuine article rather than the sound-a-like. The same will apply to voiceovers. Just because you sound like a celebrity it doesn't mean that clients will pay celebrity prices for your voice.

There could be a market with smaller areas like ringtones, customised audio cards and so on, but again this won't be at celebrity rates, this will be normal voice rates and the work is unlikely to flood in. Also beware of positioning yourself as a sound-a-like as rules will apply. If you're unfairly poaching work from a celebrity, their agent may look into the legal side of things and claim for lost revenue.

However sounding "similar" to a celebrity is a good place to be when a celebrity is popular. Celebs will come in and out of fashion but there is certainly money to be made if you can position yourself as an affordable alternative. Dervla Kirwin made a big splash voicing the sexy sounding M&S ads on TV and many people have since cast for a new commercial along the lines of "someone like that lady off the food ads".

So instead of trying to sound like a celebrity, why not adapt your demos to reflect current trends? Whatever seems hot at the moment, try to get a sample of yourself doing a similar style without labelling yourself as a copycat. Often being a sound-a-like can cheapen your brand, but being a versatile voice who can adapt their style could prove more profitable.

1.16 Why would an advertising agency use a celebrity voice instead of mine?

Big advertising agencies are full of creative people who sell to the mass public, but in the same way, the ad agencies have to sell their ideas to big companies first. Making a pitch with a celebrity voice can really help sell an idea, as the famous voice is effectively a product in its own right. This means that when they walk into a pitch, the end client will have a stronger mental picture of the commercial if they already know the voice. You could string out a long sentence trying to explain that you'll use a down-to-earth Northern voice, a bit cheeky, some humourous tone, abit of a clown and so on. The client will sit there and try to imagine this guy. Or you could say "we'll use Peter Kay" and the client can instantly hear Peter Kay reading the tagline in his head.

Also we have a preconceived image of a celebrity which the product being sold can inherit. Stephen Fry is considered to be quintessentially English and this has been utilised by many brands such as Twinings Tea.

Celebrity voices can be expensive so the choice to use one is normally only an option for large companies with big budgets. But if the budget allows for it, why not use a celebrity voice for all of the above reasons?

Chapter 2

Basic Business

2.1   How much will it cost to start up as a voiceover?

Start up costs are a considerable barrier of entry into the market for an aspiring voiceover but let's assume you already have a telephone/mobile, home computer with printer, broadband internet, and of course a cuddly toy. If you're setting up your own home recording facilities and you want to make money as a professional voiceover, then you must be prepared to invest the money to set up a professional studio.

There are always exceptions such as if you can gain access to a friend's/work studio but for the sake of this question we'll assume this is not the case.

You'll need to consider:

- Microphone with pop shield and stand – Your most important investment. Best options would be a mic such as the Neumann TLM103 which costs in the region of £800.

- Soundproof recording environment – A professional setup would be around £3,000 for a small ready-made booth and additional sound conditioning.

- Associated recording software from £0–£500.

- Associated recording hardware such as pre-amp/headphone amp, mixing desk, cabling from £500–£1,000.

- A good pair of headphones such as DT 100s from £90–£110.

- ISDN codec and ISDN line rental (only applicable if you want to be an ISDN voice) – Codec around £1,000 and rental cost around £50 a month.

- Fax machine – You can get a virtual fax-to-email number for about £10–£50 a year.

You'll also need to put some budget aside for marketing. Depending on your web abilities, you may need help setting up a website. This could be £500–£3,000 – it's up to you how extravagant you want to be with bells and possibly whistles too. Your demo will cost you more time than money, so familiarise yourself with editing software and you can do it yourself. Some aspiring voiceovers will enlist the help of a showreel production company which may cost £100 upwards. To get your name out there you need to market yourself. Many voices will pay for one or two internet directories, postal marketing and web ads – let's say £500–£1,000. You might also want to brand your marketing and invoices with some headed paper which could be another £250 for logo design and printing costs.

So initial start up costs will commonly be in the region of £5,500–£11,000 in your first 12 months. Once your studio is up and running, overheads aren't generally high as it's a home-based business.

Of course, in business there are no guarantees of success so investments in your business are a risk.

If you're starting out as a "jobbing" voiceover based in or around a local studio you can avoid the initial outlay of costs that home voiceovers have. However it's a lot more difficult to break into this market if you have no previous experience and your time and investment will be spent on training and showreel production costs. If you're lucky enough to be taken under the wing of an agency then you'll find a lot of these costs may be covered as the agency will be investing in you.

2.2   Can I set myself up as a limited company?

This is advice best given by an accountant on a case by case basis. Many voiceover artists, especially those making a healthy salary, will set themselves up as a limited company. Because your business is just you it does not mean that you have to operate as a sole trader. Due to personal tax bands, it's sometimes more efficient to offer your services through a limited company. In addition it can look more professional and help establish your brand.

Running a limited company can be more complex than being a sole trader, so as mentioned, please take advice from your accountant.

If you do choose to set yourself up as a limited company we'd advise choosing a company name that's based on your professional name to avoid confusion and to reinforce your brand.

2.3   Do I need an accountant?

If you're confident doing your own accounts and they're pretty straightforward, you can easily run your business without paying an accountant. For small sole traders, an accountant's fees normally start from around £200+VAT for the year so can be covered after a couple of corporate jobs. We'd recommend having an accountant simply so you have more time to focus on other aspects of your work. You'll also find an accountant may be able to spot other tax considerations you had not initially thought of, such as depreciation on your studio equipment and use of home as office. You may find your accountant's fees are being covered simply by his or her expertise. If there are any changes to the law or important considerations then you can rest assured that your accountant will inform you. Please be aware that if your revenue (not profit) is over a certain amount, it's mandatory that you become VAT registered.

If your business grows, your accountant can also advise whether it's better for you to become incorporated. If you leave this decision, you may find you've been paying more tax than you need to.

We'd advise using a local accountant who you can meet face to face, and who is perhaps recommended by word of mouth. Although an accountant won't administer your day-to-day book-keeping, they can normally advise how to set this up efficiently so that you can obtain useful statistics.

Some accountants will share their knowledge and give you tips on how you can improve the profitability of your business based on the information they've gleaned from their other clients.

2.4   Is it a good idea to have my own standard terms and conditions?

Don't gloss over this area, because if you subsequently hit issues you'll be in a better legal position. Your standard terms and conditions should clarify your re-record policy, payment terms, cancellation policy, breach of usage, copyright, liability etc. You can also include other beneficial terms such as automatically gaining permission to use recordings and/or client names in your marketing/demo audio. Please refer to our sample set of terms and conditions and feel free to adapt for your own use (Appendix A).

If you formalise your booking procedure you can include these terms and conditions in a booking form, which the client signs to agree the work. Whatever you do, ensure they are agreed prior to recording – don't just put them on your invoice.

If your terms are reasonable and clear, then you should have no problem enforcing them if required; for example, invoicing for a cancellation fee or refusing a third free re-record. If the client becomes awkward then the advice is to keep calm, consider small compromises and highlight the fact that your terms and conditions were accepted when they confirmed the booking. If the client remains hostile and they refuse to pay an invoice, consider following the small claims procedure online at www.moneyclaim.gov.uk. We've known some unhappy clients who will quote the 'distance selling regulations' and request a refund. These regulations do not apply to business-to-business deals and customised products such as a recording of a client's script are also exempt.

In addition to your terms and conditions, do remember anything agreed on the phone may be easily disputed. Instead, try to keep as much correspondence on email, so you have a paper trail to prove your position.

2.5   How do I license my voice recordings?

Most voiceover recordings are not sold, but instead, licensed for use. In practice, a lot of voiceover artists supply their recordings but are vague about where the recordings are licensed for. However, even small recordings should have some sort of default licence statement, even if it allows unlimited use of the recordings for the particular project. For example when invoicing for a local radio recording, include a statement such as "licensed for broadcast on [radio station name] for 12 months from initial transmission". Even better would be to reference start and end dates if you have this information.

If a recording could potentially have high exposure, then you must agree a licence for use when you agree the rate. In these situations ensure a formal booking agreement, which indicates the licence, is signed by the client prior to the recording/session.

Please view our sample licence agreement (Appendix B) which you are free to adapt for your own use.

Ensure that your booking agreement specifies that you can recover licence fees if you find that your licence has been breached. If this happens, you can then legitimately follow the small claims procedure (see online at www.moneyclaim.gov.uk). Additionally, if you're an Equity member, they may be able to support you.

If your licence has a time limit, such as 12 months, then you should make a diary entry for the week before expiry to follow up and see whether further usage/licences are required.

2.6   What payment methods should I accept?

Most voiceovers are freelance and will generate invoices requesting payment for the work they've completed (see Appendix D for a sample invoice). Your invoices should state the methods of payment you accept.

Companies are increasingly paying by BACS or bank transfer rather than the traditional cheque run. The benefit of this is that many banks now offer "Faster Payments Service" (FPS) as standard. This will transfer money almost instantly from one account to another, meaning you can request your money and could see it in your account within 30 minutes. CHAPS transfers are also often same-day but there are generally fees attached to these so they're not preferable for the client.

We recommend you sign up for a PayPal account, which is very useful for producers based in other countries. PayPal will deduct fees, so build these into your quotes rather than surprising the client with additional costs when you invoice. You can also accept credit/debit cards via a service like Google Checkout. Both of these are great methods and give an instant indication that the client has paid, so are very useful if you're requesting prepayment.

If you do accept money via PayPal, be wary of scam emails which try to obtain your login details. One tip is never to click on emails which appear to be from PayPal or other banks/authorities. A few voiceovers have found their PayPal accounts compromised, usually because they clicked a link in an email which took them to a fake PayPal site. We recommend if you see an email which requires action, open a browser and visit the official PayPal website, without clicking on links within the email.

2.7 What additional considerations are there when invoicing an overseas client?

The first consideration is whether to offer them credit at all! Unless you have a good history with an overseas client, we recommend you ask them to prepay before providing services.

If you are offering credit, ensure that you include your international payment information on your invoices. This may be just your PayPal address, or if you're accepting bank transfers, include your IBAN and BIC/SWIFT code. It's also a good idea to include the currency that your bank account is in and your bank address.

If you're VAT registered and you're invoicing a European client, then you may find you do not need to add VAT and can instead quote their VAT number. For companies outside the EU, VAT is not applicable. Some anomalies exist; transactions in the Isle of Man are currently exempt from VAT and situations do change, so we recommend you check www.hmrc.gov.uk for the latest official guidelines.

Please be aware that you should invoice in the currency agreed when providing the quote. You may find it easier to keep to GBP but understand that some clients may need to fix their costs in their own currency, and if so, be aware that exchange rates fluctuate and ensure you build in some contingency if you have any hard/fixed costs.

You may also want to consider accepting credit/debit card payments using a service such as Google Checkout.

When you quote, ensure this is inclusive of all charges. It's your responsibility to cover costs of PayPal or bank transfer fees.

2.8   How do I make sure that I'm paid for my work?

There are many resources online to help you recover your money. If you search for "Business Link debt recovery" it will take you to a page listing methods of recovering unpaid sums of money.

However you don't want it to reach this stage, so firstly make sure you consider the following:

- Get to know your customers – Run a credit check on any new customers wishing to place a large booking with you. It's not cost effective to do this on small jobs, but it could save you time and money down the line on the larger jobs. Also, work on building rapport and trust as you're less likely to be let down if you have a good relationship with them.

- Make them aware of your payment terms and conditions – Include your payment terms as standard. Make this clear, and not in the small print, so there's no confusion.

- Get them to sign a booking form – This should list the job/licence you've agreed in principle and be accompanied by your terms and conditions.

- Keep your conversations/enquiries on email rather than telephone – This sounds pedantic, but if you don't have a copy of the conversation, you have no proof of what was agreed.

- Practise good housekeeping – Send your invoices regularly, immediately after each job if possible. If you send invoices late, they'll be processed late.

- Get someone else to do your accounts/invoices – Going back to the personal relationship you have with your clients, it's often easier if a spouse or professional deals with the paperwork. A good cop, bad cop approach when chasing money.

- Offer incentives to customers who pay early – This can be something like a small discount for prepayment or reliable payers.

- Have a system in place to track overdue invoices – Don't just forget about an invoice, then six months down the line furiously chase an unpaid job. Paperwork can on occasion get lost, so have a system that tracks overdue invoices each month. Send a friendly reminder if a job goes unpaid as it can prompt a client to say they didn't receive the invoice initially.

- Set a credit limit – It's sensible to have a standard credit limit for your customers. If they have invoices due that meet your credit limit, explain that you cannot accept more work until the older invoices are paid. Most companies will be fine with this as long as you make it clear from the start that you have a credit limit in place.

- Be patient with regular clients – Don't immediately blacklist someone if they don't meet your 30 day terms. Money issues can easily upset people, so take a soft approach at first, especially with your regular customers. Sending them a court summons for a £40 job that's five days overdue may not be wise in the long run...

- Small claims procedure – This isn't as daunting as it may sound. You can do this online and the cost will depend on the size of the claim. This will often prompt a client to pay up to avoid any court action.

- Debt collection – It's not pleasant if it gets to this stage. Usually a court will instruct a debt collector, if the small claims procedure awards in your favour. Debt collectors can take a cut of their collection, so be aware of their terms and conditions before you go down this route.

- Ask for prepayment from sole traders and companies overseas – It can be tricky to recover money from a sole trader or an overseas company; the best advice is to have a prepayment system in place. Please see Question 2.6 "What payment methods should I accept?" for some suggestions on prepayment options. If you don't ask for prepayment, then you must accept there's a risk.

2.9   Can I set up my studio on a budget?

If you're making an income from voiceover work, then it's a good idea to invest in a full setup without compromising on quality. You'll find a more detailed list of studio essentials in Question 5.3 "What studio equipment will I need?".

However if you're starting from scratch and testing the water, we recommend that you buy less equipment to start with, rather than cheaper equipment. This will maintain quality control and also prevent you having to replace the whole setup when business develops. You can get an adequate amateur setup for less than £1,000, assuming that you have broadband internet and a home computer/laptop to work with.

You first important purchase will be your microphone and you can't take a budget approach on this. Rather than buying a cheap USB microphone, we suggest investing in a proper XLR microphone that's suited to voiceover work. XLR describes the three-pin connector on the microphone rather than it having a USB connection. You can't go wrong with a Neumann TLM 103. You can buy one new for around £800, but shop around on auction sites and you may pick up a second hand bargain first. A good microphone will pick up everything, so you'll need to ensure you put some effort into creating a soundproof environment. Please see Question 5.8 "What's the cheapest way to create a soundproof studio?". To plug your microphone into your computer you'll then need an "XLR to USB" connector. These are about £30. Great, you now have a microphone plugged into your computer... what next?

Along with the microphone you'll need a stand to hold the microphone and a pop shield. You can get these for around £15 each.

Your next important investment will be your headphones. You need a pair of professional headphones such as DT100s to be able to assess your recording quality; you won't hear the nasties on cheap headphones. These are around £90–£110 brand new but again you can shop for a second hand pair.

You can download a free audio software package for your computer such as "Audacity" to begin with.

The whole setup will come to around £900–£1,000 if you shop wisely, and equips you with good headphones and a good microphone attached to your home PC. Not bad for a starter kit but you WILL need to invest more if you want to take it more seriously.

2.10   How do I keep motivated?

When beginning any new venture, it's crucial that you remain motivated to follow it through to the desired result. In this case the desired result is to establish yourself as a voiceover and build on your client base.

- Mission statement and targets – Start by writing a mission statement of what you are trying to achieve and set targets along the way. These might be goals such as setting up your own website, learning to record and edit yourself and so on.

- Discipline – It's good to keep refreshing your to do list with any new jobs that crop up so things don't slip by, but try to tick them off in order of oldest first. It's not always possible of course as some will be more critical than others, but if you don't follow this pattern you'll find that you keep leaving the "boring" jobs; eventually you'll get to a point where you have a whole list of boring jobs that you don't feel like tackling. It's a great feeling when you can tick off a killer job on your list.

- Keep a diary of development – Don't just tick off your jobs list and forget about them, keep track of what you've achieved in a diary. It's nice to look back and see how you've developed from the start.

- Anticipate seasonal trends – Being a self-employed voiceover means that you will see peaks and troughs in work. You may experience lulls around the festive period or dips over Easter/summer holidays as clients take leave. You may find work picks up at the end of the financial year as companies burn budgets up. You might then find dips at the start of the new financial year when businesses are looking after money. Be sensible and plan for these, but don't be disheartened.

- Remember why – Remind yourself of why you're doing this. If it's simply a cash motivated business then have reminders of what the money is for such as your family or a treat for yourself like a holiday. If the venture is because you want to escape an old job or be your own boss, keep reminders of how much more enjoyable it is to have the freedom of doing work that you really want to do. Enjoy it!

2.11   How do I know it's working?

Whatever your business, it's vital that you monitor your success as best as you can. The only way to expand your business is to capitalise on the areas that are working well and to adapt in the areas that need improving.

One sign that it's working is that you'll find your clients continue to book work with you. This is a clear display of their faith in your ability to deliver and their acceptance of your fees.

You'll also find that your client list will begin to grow as your business develops. This is hopefully due to the great marketing you're doing as well as helpful "word of mouth" recommendations. If you build a client database it's easy to see this as it increases. It's important that you monitor where people found you. If you're paying £100 a month for internet adverts, but your clients are finding you through simple search result placement of your own website, then you could be wasting your money on those adverts.

You should make sure that you monitor your sales and bottom line figures too! It won't tell you where the bookings came from but it's easier to chart and see clear trends.

There are other hints that it's working such as receiving Christmas cards from producers who value their relationship with you. You might also find clients are searching for you by name because of a recent campaign and they want to bag "the voice from THAT commercial".

Finally, you'll find that the voiceover world is pretty small and most voiceovers are aware of the major players. Successful voiceovers will have a reputation amongst their peers, so if you find your reputation growing, you're doing something right!

2.12   Should I sign up for an exclusivity contract?

If you are asked to agree to anything which involves exclusivity, tread carefully and ensure you know exactly what the implications are.

Some voice agencies request exclusivity, and this can mean that all your work would need to go via them. This can be restrictive and frankly annoying if you are getting good work from your own marketing efforts, but still having a percentage taken away. Try to exempt areas where the agency would not generally market you (such as local radio, small corporate scripts etc.), as this would be a good compromise for both parties.

In addition, some clients ask for exclusivity in certain projects. For example you may be signed up as the new voice of a mobile network, and the network wants to ensure you do not work with any of its competitors. This is beneficial for them but you should ensure such a contract is not loosely defined. Get them to list the company names instead of just defining "other mobile companies", otherwise you may find you have to decline other opportunities such as a commercial for a mobile phone store. Once it's clear what you can and can't do, it's important to estimate how much work you could lose based on recent bookings.

A client should pay extra for exclusivity or pay a "retainer" fee so that you are getting a regular income throughout the duration of the contract, even if they aren't giving you work. Also check the get-out clauses. Some voices will include a clause that states if they have not had any bookings for a period of time, 12 months say, then they can opt out of the contract and the exclusivity.

Chapter 3

Branding and Marketing

3.1   How do I define my brand?

It's important to decide how you'd describe your voice and where you fit into the market. If a producer wrote a voice brief on a script in a single line what would be the description that would get you shouting "That's me!"?

A good exercise is to write down up to ten words or short phrases, in order of importance, that describe your voice. These voice qualities may describe your age, style, pitch, accent, timbre etc. These are your "voice qualities".

Next do a similar exercise and write down up to ten words or short phrases that describe the qualities not related to your voice, such as turn around time, studio access, attitude, pricing etc. These are your "non-voice qualities".

The qualities identified will affect which search terms you target for internet searches, what images and text you use in mail outs and which samples you use on demo audio. It even affects how you deal with your clients and should influence how other voiceovers perceive you. Being consistent across all your interactions will reinforce your brand.

You may like to decide on a particular font that you always use. Consider creating a logo, which may just be your name in this font. If you have a website, the look and feel as well as the images used should reflect your brand qualities. Once you've established that brand, maintain it as this is what people will be looking out for when searching for you. If you have a great logo on headed paper but don't brand your demo CD, producers will lose the CD in a pile.

3.2   Should I have a website?

Nowadays a web presence is essential. The internet is used by creatives when thinking about initial ideas, right through to producers who are choosing the voices.

You can have a web presence without maintaining your own website through the use of web directories, YouTube and even profile pages and groups on social networking sites. For example getting featured on Voiceovers.co.uk allows exposure to an already established community of producers. Directories will normally have more marketing budget than a single voiceover so you may get more hits for your money.

However some reasons for having your own website include:

- You can have a professional email address, rather than a free Hotmail, Gmail or Yahoo? account.

- You indicate to potential clients that you're an established and full-time voiceover.

- You reinforce your own brand image. For example a full-time cartoon voiceover may have a playful cartoon image of themselves.

- You have more control over the focus of your work. You can display as many demos as you like and include pictures of your professional studio amongst other things.

- You improve exposure via internet search hits.

Maintaining a website can be a lot of work if you don't have the know-how and can be costly. If your website is not updated regularly then it can actually have a negative impact on your image. Instead, consider redirecting your website to your directory profile on another website, one that you do maintain. You will still benefit from having your own email address.

3.3   Do I need a voiceover agent?

Thirty or more years ago, voiceover agents were used almost exclusively when booking voiceover recordings. With the advent of new media and the internet, many companies are finding that going through a traditional agency is sometimes not feasible, mainly due to budgets.

Currently, many voiceover artists are earning a living without an agent so you don't necessarily need a voiceover agent to be successful in the industry. However a voiceover agent still holds the key to more lucrative work, such as national TV campaigns. This is generally because the London advertising agencies don't need to compromise on voice costs and therefore find it more convenient to go to one or two voice agents than to contact many voiceover artists directly.

There are good and bad voiceover agents, so don't assume that just because you are on the books of an agency, it will lead to guaranteed work. It can be very difficult to get signed up by a good agency and it's probably essential to be based in London or at least within commuting distance. If you have a unique selling point and a good reputation for what you do, then you may find that you do not need an agent.

An agent will take care of most of the "business" side of being a voiceover artist; their skills lie in experience with contracts and negotiation. Advertising agencies like to book via an agency because the quality control has been done for them – they do not need to filter out inexperienced voices themselves. By their very nature voiceover agents have to be picky, so getting a good agent can be tough, but worthwhile.

3.4   How do I get a good voiceover agent?

Getting a good agent can be tough if you have no experience, so before you start looking, try to seal some high profile jobs yourself. If you can send an agent demos with genuine brand names, they'll have a much better chance of selling you in the commercial market.

Once you have a few agency details, check their websites for an appropriate niche for your voice. Find a way to position yourself so that you fill a gap in their books, giving you more opportunities for work. Next, see whether you are in contact with anyone on their books and ask them about the agency. Do they seem like your kind of people? If so, you can ask your voiceover friend to mention you in passing and sow the seed before introducing yourself and sending them your demo. If they hear about you from another voice they represent, it could give you more credibility.

If all goes to plan you now need to discuss with the agent which markets you will be represented in. It's likely to be the commercial market, but do they want exclusivity? Do they want it in all areas? Chat about what works best for you, as it's likely the agent won't request to represent you for minor corporate work and local radio ads, allowing you a little freedom.

If you get to this stage, you're doing very well indeed. Now you need to look at the small print of the contract, such as length of representation, any clauses and, probably most importantly to you, what percentage commission they take. Fifteen to twenty-five per cent seems standard and pretty fair for most established and trusted agencies, but more than this and you need to consider whether the work they can get you will justify this cut.

Finally, if you've been with an agent for a while and it's not working for you because of lack of work or you feel they're not pushing you enough, then look around for another. It's easier to get an agent when you already have one, as your application will be more credible from the start. There's also an element of poaching a voice from another agent which can help you in this situation. If you really do have a strong niche, then you have the best chance of obtaining a good agent who can push you for plenty of work.

You can search online for potential agents; search as if you are a producer looking for a voice and then you'll be contacting the agencies that have the best online exposure. Also get a copy of the book *Contacts* which is an annual publication by Spotlight and includes a listing of voice agents and their contact details.

3.5 How do I market myself for local radio recordings?

Firstly, you will need a demo containing commercial recordings, ideally authentic. This will display your range of styles and accents (and characters if applicable). Many producers will cast their voices online using a website such as www.voiceovers.co.uk; however there are various other ways for you to market yourself on top of this. Availability emails are helpful as many producers will prioritise voices with good availability.

Another good way to get your name known is by attending "VOX", an annual conference in the UK which specialises in the commercial production market. This conference is attended by many independent producers, producers from radio stations and other voice artists.

It would be worthwhile contacting UK radio stations to ask whether they produce their commercials "in-house" and if so, whether they would like to receive your demo CD. When speaking to potential producers, it's important to mention your excellent availability and ISDN access and make them aware of whether you work to standard industry rates.

3.6   Should I send availability emails?

Some producers like to receive availability emails from their regular pool of voices. An availability email reminds the producer of your general availability for the upcoming week. It's normally only effective in the local radio/commercial production side of the business where quick turnaround is important. Whether or not the emails are read is almost irrelevant, as it serves mostly as a reminder of your existence. If you manually send your availability emails, it's best to use the BCC field for privacy reasons. If your list grows large, you could consider using a website to automate this process. You don't want to be seen as a spammer so ensure every email you send lets them know how they can opt out of your mailing list.

Outside of the local radio market, it's still good practice to remind clients of your services every two to three months with a friendly email, letting them know you're still generally available for work.

3.7   How   do   I   get   a   good   internet   search   placement?

An internet search placement refers to the position of your website in the search results when somebody searches using a relevant phrase. Whether you are optimising your website yourself or getting your web design company to do it for you, deciding which phrases are most relevant to you is crucial. What is your unique selling point? Think of some key words and phrases that match your brand image. Ensure these words and phrases are included within the text on your site.

Choose a web address to reflect your voice description such as www.youngcorporatevoice.co.uk and include these words in the title of your index page. Ask your web developer if you don't understand the details here.

Another way to improve your placement is to get your web address featured on other websites such as free directories and link sites. Be sure that these sites are voiceover related and not generic or designed to improve search rankings, as it's rumoured search engines look unfavourably on this.

Other techniques to boost your position include setting your meta-data correctly, naming your pages sensibly and keeping your site up to date with new content every couple of months.

If you want an instant way to stand out in the search results, consider paying for a search engine advert.

3.8   Do I have a unique selling point?

Highlighting a unique selling point is vital for dominance in any business market-place. Unfortunately, we receive many demos where a native accent has been ditched in favour of a neutral or RP accent. If you have a unique selling point then flaunt it. This could be your native accent or it might be that you're flexible with characters, you have a rich, husky voice or that you have an ethnic sound. However your USP doesn't have to focus on your voice; it can be your location, availability, price, quality of studio. Whatever it is, it's important to exploit it!

If you're finding it hard to identify your uniqueness then the subtleties become more important. Your attitude or personality when working with clients, along with your costs, will need to put you ahead of the competition. In essence you create your own unique selling point.

3.9 How can I cultivate a good relationship with a producer/client?

After working with a producer for the first time, it's important to try to maintain the relationship, to encourage repeat bookings. From the outset, be calm, friendly, flexible with availability and fair with costs. You want to ensure a producer doesn't think it'll be difficult to deal with you again. Try to establish a rapport with the producer and check whether they would be happy to receive email updates on your availability.

Being a producer can be a stressful job with tight deadlines, so they will tend to favour voices who are easy to work with and can adapt to their schedule. Take an interest in their work, and if it's a directed session, play around with characters or accents to demonstrate your range if there's time for a pre-session chit chat. In a week or so, ask for a copy of your latest recording. It might be useful on your demo and the request could serve as another reminder.

If you're flexible with pickups then this can earn you brownie points. Many voiceovers will record the odd one or two pickup lines as a freebie if the producer has made a genuine mistake with the script or direction. Ensure your effort is representative of the potential work you might get in return.

3.10   What response will I get to my marketing?

Many people think being a voiceover is about reading scripts in a booth; however 95% of your time and effort is likely to be, and probably should be, marketing yourself.

The response you get from your marketing depends on the different activities you do. Direct mail marketing can be disheartening; if you get a response rate of 3% you should consider yourself very lucky indeed! Don't be put off by this though. Once you've started to get your brand out there, it becomes more recognisable. We've had enquiries come in from mail shots that we sent 18 months previously. Don't overdo it and harass people who obviously aren't interested, but do follow up your initial mail shot a couple of months later with a more casual reminder. Let them know you're still around and ready to work. If they clocked your branding first time round, it's likely they'll recognise it the second time.

If you get a very poor response on a mail shot, try tweaking your text or your demo audio and see whether your next mail shot is more successful.

With online marketing it is generally much easier to track response rates. Email marketing websites should not only be able to tell you how many people on your mailing list successfully received your message, but also how many opened the email and how many clicked through to see more.

You can gather great feedback using online tools such as Google Analytics which shows you a multitude of graphs and stats.

In our experience, marketing is more effective if you focus your attention on ensuring clients can find you when they need your type of voice. For example a single well-placed press release online can draw any number of producers to you, rather than you specifically targeting a finite number of producers on a mailing list.

3.11   I feel pigeon-holed. Is this bad?

If you're starting to feel pigeon-holed in a particular area, we'd actually advise jumping on this as a marketing opportunity. Possibly give the style its own demo and try to claim that you are the authority in this particular voice area. It can mean that your name is in a producer's mind as soon as they have this requirement. This can only be a good thing!

If you find you're not getting as much work as you'd like, consider branching out in a controlled way. The danger is trying to be all things to all people as this can dilute your brand identity. See Question 3.17 "How do I expand into new markets?".

3.12   How should I choose my email address?

Clever configuration of your email addresses by yourself or your web guru can help prevent spam and allow you to track which marketing is working. We'd advise setting up a private email address, your "master" email address which you do not pass to anyone or publish anywhere. Then set up a range of email "aliases" which forward to this master address. By using a different alias on each marketing campaign or a different email address per web directory you can track where your enquiries are coming from. If you start receiving spam you can choose to deactivate this alias and set up a new one.

We'd advise having your own domain name rather than creating multiple hotmail accounts (or other free email services) as it will appear more professional. You can buy a domain from a registrar such as www.123-reg.co.uk. Once registered, most companies offer a control panel which will allow you to either set up email forwarding or purchase a POP mailbox. When you choose an email address, ensure you pick a suitable name that's on brand rather than "fluffyjumpers69@...".

Please be aware that if your email address appears in plain text on a website, you are likely to start receiving spam after a period of time. Instead, consider displaying your email address as an image.

3.13   How do I build a mailing list?

We're often asked whether we have databases of producers that voiceovers can email their demos to. Most producers are very busy and inundated with demos so may find an unrequested email irrelevant at best. If a set of email addresses are easily obtainable, the likelihood is that they're already overused and of little value.

A good method to create your own mailing list would be to send suitable companies a letter and ask them whether they use voiceover artists and would they be interested in receiving your demo or availability emails. See Question 3.14 "What should I include in a marketing letter?".

Established voiceovers will create a list of email addresses from clients who have enquired or booked them in the past and this is a great way to grow your own mailing list. It's good practice to remind clients that you exist if they haven't used you for a few months. Have a column in your database which logs the last time they used you.

Try to avoid sending unsolicited marketing emails to new contacts. It's more acceptable and more effective to draw producers to contact you first and subsequently remind them of your services.

3.14   What should I include in a marketing letter?

Visualise a busy producer opening yet another voiceover marketing letter. In the same way that your demo needs to sell you in the first 30 seconds, your letter needs to be direct to spoon-feed the key points that make you workable. Refer to Question 3.1 "How do I define my brand?" for a few tips.

The first short paragraph of your letter should outline your native accent, your studio situation, your normal availability and what makes you unique. We're not talking about an essay – 50 words is probably adequate.

Next, if you're targeting a particular market, such as local radio, it's best to mention how you work out your rates. For example do you work to Equity rates?

In the next paragraph, promote yourself as a person who is easy to work with, such as being able to offer free auditions.

If you have previous clients in the target market, include a couple of these names to give yourself credibility.

If you're not including a demo CD (which is best avoided on large campaigns due to cost), let them know where they can hear your samples and find out more about you. If you have headed paper, use it, as this can send a much more professional message.

If you're an actor, don't just send your standard paper CV and headshot photo as it's irrelevant. The only CV you need is your demo audio which should include copies of your previous work.

3.15 Do I include a photo on my marketing/website?

This is a common question and in nearly all cases the answer is no. A photo gives a preconceived idea as to how your voice sounds or should sound. We hear many stories of healthy client relationships suddenly stopping when the client meets or sees a picture of the voice.

Some voiceovers can retain a youthful voice even when their looks would indicate they'd be more appropriate advertising incontinence pants! There is an exception and that's when your looks complement your voice and brand image, so they will positively impact on your work.

We recommend that if you're starting out, definitely do not include a picture. Let your voice sell you.

3.16   How do I get my foot in the door?

It's useful to look at some established voiceover artists and see how they entered the industry. There are some interesting stories and some show the age old adage of "it's who you know, not what you know" to be true.

We find many voiceover artists have previously had a part-time or full-time job in a related industry first, and this has been key to breaking into the voiceover world. At a recent voiceover conference, of the voices we surveyed, more than 90% had previously worked in a media related industry.

Some media jobs provide access to professional studios, allow opportunities for experimenting in voiceover recordings or put you amongst key decision makers/producers.

Some examples are:

- Being a radio presenter where you'll have great studio access and contact with producers.

- Working at a production company where you'll have opportunities to experiment in voiceover recordings and influence end clients. You'll also get the chance to sit in on voice sessions and be able to hear clients giving direction, as well as form your own opinion on what does and doesn't work and eventually give direction yourself.

- Working at a voice or advertising agency where you'll be interacting with casting directors and may be asked to try out or provide a guide track.

- Working with another voiceover artist where you'll be able to pick up voiceover tips and share studio access.

If you find it difficult to get a job in these areas, consider joining a group, such as hospital radio, to get some free experience in front of a microphone.

Some will use their acting experience to help them break into the voiceover industry; however with a large number of actors and a lack of studio access, it may not be the easiest route.

3.17 How do I expand into new markets?

If you're predominantly focused on one or two areas such as voice recordings for radio and television commercials, then it's worth considering trying to expand into other market areas.

How do I expand into...?:

- Radio commercials – Ensure that you have a separate demo dedicated to commercial recordings. Have great availability and consider sending availability update emails. Radio commercials normally pay low fees but are high in quantity so are suited to voiceovers who have their own studio facilities, ideally with ISDN connectivity.

- National television commercials – A lot of TV work is still booked via the big voice agencies, so submit your demo to these agents and try to get on their books. If you have a unique selling point or a niche voice you have the best chance of success. Look at styles of other voices on their books, find a gap you can fill and pigeon hole yourself when you send your demo to them.

- Documentaries – Like national television commercials, many documentary companies will have their regular suppliers so research these agents and send off your demo. However if you've little or no experience in this area, record some test audio and approach the millions of amateur and small time documentary makers who are all over the internet. Carve out your own documentary style which for many voices is their most natural sound.

- Corporate work – Having relevant demo audio is a must as this is a very different style. The corporate market is huge, but due to budgets, it's normally advisable that you have your own studio facilities and you're comfortable with recording and editing larger scripts yourself. In many cases you may deal direct with the end client so quality control is very important. Try to build up a relationship with companies who provide corporate and telephone audio for their end clients. Ensure the relationship is win/win by setting your rates so that they can make a healthy profit too. When considering targeting the IVR market (telephone menu systems) you might wonder, "Where are the men?" Well yes, it does seem to favour female voices, so if you're male don't assume there's a huge niche to be filled by male voices. The reason for this is that many telephone systems will often sound clearer with voices at the higher end of the vocal range. Bassy male voices can come across muffled, unclear and unfriendly, so tend to be used much less on these recordings.

- Continuity – Continuity jobs don't arise very often. Station voices are carefully selected and the contracts will indicate ongoing work. If you've had experience presenting on radio or television, this can put you in a good position as you'll be asked to write the copy as well as read it. If you're not used to constructing these small "links", it can be a tricky job. Put together a demo of intros to shows using a TV guide and send it off to the station producers. The shifts can be around eight hours if performed live, so you'll need to make sure it won't impact on customers who use you for last minute bookings. It's important to put your stamp on this live announcing as it's an opportunity to demonstrate your personality and can really help create a recognisable brand.

Your demo audio is the most important part of your marketing, so when breaking into new areas, put the effort into the samples you send. Having relevant samples is key! Take time to create specific demos like roleplay audio, telephone prompts and technical tutorials. Your clients are in turn probably selling you to their end clients so make it easy for them by giving them a variety to choose between.

3.18   Should I try to break into my local area before launching myself nationally or globally?

A focus on your local or regional companies when you are launching yourself can be a wise decision, as it gives you a chance to establish yourself and build a portfolio. Target companies who have their own studio recording facilities as they will invariably prefer to direct and record a voice in person rather than remotely, and you can foster a relationship with them. The danger is trying to run before you can walk and sending an underdeveloped demo nationally. As your work and portfolio expands, so should your marketing reach.

Having an online presence will allow you an instant global audience and first impressions last a long time, so think about this advice before you jump in with a big website push.

3.19   Should I define my own ethical policy?

Some voiceover artists don't wish to voice scripts for specific companies or topics. This is entirely your decision and in some cases it can protect your brand image.

Do you voice for sex lines? Do you want to advertise such services?

Would you be happy promoting gambling websites? How about misleading telephone competition scripts?

Whatever your thoughts, take some time to define what you are comfortable voicing and write your own ethical policy, before you are put on the spot.

You do not necessarily have to publish your policy. The most important thing is to have given it some thought before questions are asked.

3.20   What is online auditioning, and should I do it?

There are many websites that you can join who offer "easy casting" for clients. This generally means that the client can submit a new job to an online notice board. They'll explain the job, the usage and the type of voice they want. Then it's up to you to submit a test sample or audition from their script along with the fee you'd charge if they selected you.

Unfortunately, much of this work will be awarded to the lowest bidder. Many voices on these types of websites are not full-time voices so they may not be familiar with common rates. There's also the issue with quality control as anybody can record a couple of samples on a cheap computer microphone and set up their "virtual shop front" as a voiceover artist. It's up to the client to listen out for sound quality on the auditions but of course not everybody notices a poor recording.

These websites are by no means all bad though and are also used to cast some large jobs. There's also the perspective of the amateur voiceover who can be pitched next to an established voice with no pre-judgement, as they're just two equal candidates in the eyes of the client. Use it as a starting point to help you build up a healthy demo reel of genuine material.

Success rates can be very low on these sites as you may be one of 30 or 50 voices who have auditioned for a particular job. Don't be disheartened if you don't get selected for the majority of the work that you try out for. Remember a failed audition is still an opportunity for someone to hear how you sound. You may not be suitable for that particular project but you could be perfect for a job that's just around the corner.

3.21   How do I send an email for mass marketing?

For small contact groups such as your regular "availability updates" that are sent to existing clients, it's usually easiest to use your basic email software such as Microsoft Outlook. These emails are more about information to customers who already use you, so keep it simple. Just use your brand of font that you normally use and have a personal signature with a small logo.

In Microsoft Office Outlook 2007 you can create a mailing list easily. Select "Contacts" on the left tab menu then click the arrow next to "New" and from the drop down menu click "Distribution List". A box opens allowing you to name the group, and click the "Add New" button to add each email address you wish to include. Save this and when you want to email this group just type the group name in the address field of the email.

When sending an email to a mailing list from Outlook or a basic email program, it's good practice to keep your contacts hidden from each other. So in the "To" field type your own email address, then type the name of the mailing list in the "BCC" field. BCC means Blind Carbon Copy and any recipient in the BCC field will only see your email address in the "To" field and not the other recipients.

For larger contact groups, such as marketing emails sent to a database of contacts, it's often best to use a tailored "mass" email website. An example that we've used in the past is www.verticalresponse.com but these companies generally offer a very similar service.

They allow you to create an email database of contacts. You can add email contacts manually or import them from a spreadsheet and they'll store the contacts for you. These can then be split into different mailing lists such as "radio producers", "web designers" and so on.

Once you've decided on your content (text and images) you can draft an email a few ways. Most mass email services allow you to create an email by:

A) An email wizard offering pre-designed templates where you simply add a logo, images and text.
B) A basic white canvas where you can add text, logos, frames and images by clicking various options from a palette at the side of the page.
C) Writing directly in HTML code.

They'll ensure that regardless of your ability on a computer, you can create a professional message to send to your clients. Most will also provide you with HTML code that you can copy and paste onto your own website, displaying a "sign up" box for people to join your mailing list. They will also automate "opt out" requests.

For more information try searching online for this term:
    mass email marketing

3.22   Should I have a "stage name"?

Some voice artists will use a pseudonym or "professional name" for their voiceover career. This is often because their real name does not reflect their brand. If you are a producer scanning for a bubbly young female voice who would you click on first, "Edith Brown", or "Kerry Pink"?

For example, if you are a Scottish voiceover you may want to consider changing your surname to a typical Scottish sounding name... McSomething. Stereotypical we appreciate, but common sense.

Another reason for using a pseudonym is when your real name is already being used by another voiceover or actor. You may also find you need an alternative name when registering with Equity if someone else is already registered with your name.

Chapter 4

Demos

4.1   What should I put on my demo reel?

The best demo reel is normally a montage of recent work. It serves as an audio portfolio so always try to get copies of your best work. If you have no previous experience, please see Question 4.4 "What do I put on my demo if I have no previous experience?".

Ensure you highlight your unique selling point. What are you bringing to the voiceover industry? Your clips on your demo should be recorded in a professional environment and if you have access to your own studio, include some dry audio to demonstrate your studio quality. The first 30 seconds of each demo are the most crucial, so bear this in mind when choosing the running order. Most voices like to start the demo with the style which is most lucrative for them; we suggest creating distinct demos for each area that you work in, such as commercial, documentary, corporate narration, character voices, continuity, etc. This means a producer can go directly to the demo which relates to the project being cast. Demos will generally be 60–90 seconds per category.

If you make undirected recordings in your home studio then having samples of your different styles is a must. Clients are then able to indicate the style they want for their recording, avoiding any confusion and reducing the risk of having to re-record.

4.2   How do I distribute my demo?

CDs are fast becoming redundant and the majority of voices will distribute or make demos available as MP3s. Add all your demos to your own website, if you have one, along with any internet directories you're a member of. You can then direct people to your demos by including a link on an email or mail shot. You can also attach your MP3 demos to an email but it's best to ensure the total size of your emails doesn't exceed 3MB including all attachments.

If you're doing a mail shot and want to send your demos on a CD, we'd recommend using blank CD-Rs that you can burn on demand. You can get your CD-Rs branded with your logo and contact details, changing the content for each mail out. This will give you more flexibility than getting a few hundred copies of your CD replicated, which you'll be unable to change.

4.3   Why should I get copies of my work?

An established voiceover's demo becomes not only an illustration of their vocal talents, but also serves as a portfolio of credible work. A producer needs to have confidence that you are actively being used on a regular basis and for this reason it's essential that you obtain copies of your best work. Make it part of your routine to ask for a copy, and although some producers will forget, you'll slowly build up a selection of clips that you can consider to revise your demo audio. Get copies of the final mix down of your work, and at the same time make it clear that you want a copy for inclusion on your showreel, thus obtaining permission. It's a good idea to constantly evaluate your demo reel and replace with the strongest clips every few weeks if possible. Once a year fully review all your demos to make sure you're showing yourself at your best.

Some voiceovers include a line in their standard terms and conditions that allows them to use the recordings on their demo.

Look on YouTube and other websites that feature productions you've voiced, and consider embedding or linking to them on your own website.

4.4   What do I put on my demo if I have no previous experience?

If you're starting out you'll need audio samples that demonstrate your range and abilities and, if you have one, the quality of your own studio. It would be misleading if you recorded samples that mentioned company or brand names unless these reads are authentic.

Consider the following styles when creating demo audio:

- Commercial – Think about the types of products or services that you think suit your voice. Actively listen to as many commercials in these areas on websites like YouTube.com. You'll then have a good starting point to write your own scripts for some fictitious companies. Aim for five or six reads that demonstrate differing speeds and styles and that total around 60–90 seconds.

- Corporate – Look at the "about us" pages on a few websites and mock up a couple of your own. In addition, you can dig out an old help manual for an electrical item or software program with generic "press this then press that" lines to create a tutorial style read. This should be around 1.5–2 minutes in length.

- Documentary – http://search.creativecommons.org/ is a great resource to find material that you're allowed to use on your demo. For example if you search "Yorkshire" you can find text about the county that you can use to create a Yorkshire documentary sample.

- Telephone/IVR – Write a couple of "thank you for calling, please hold" lines and menu options: "press one for accounts" etc.

- Character voices, accents and impersonations – Unless these are amazing, including them can be a mistake. Don't feel you have to be a jack of all trades. A common idea is to link your characters in conversation throughout the demo. This can keep the listener interested for longer and also give the clips a purpose rather than being a random selection of character sound bites.

- Poems, book readings and singing – These are not generally appropriate for a voiceover demo.

See our sample scripts in Appendix C.

4.5   Shall I produce my first demo myself?

There are many showreel production companies that will happily help you record and produce your demo. They'll provide scripts and give you a completed product, created using their experience and knowledge of the industry. You're also likely to be recorded in a professional environment.

However if you have your own studio and you're confident producing your own demo, there are some advantages. You'll be able to source your own scripts that work with your brand/voice, you can work on your demo in your own time, and the samples will be representative of the audio quality that your clients will receive. It also means that your demo will be unique; as you haven't created it from stock scripts and music.

With a self-created demo you will have all the original sets of recordings which allows you to subsequently modify the order, swap old clips for new and generally revise until you find you get the best response from your marketing.

There are some basic rules such as starting the demo with the start of a script and ending the demo with the end of a script. Not rocket science, but it gives the demo a feel of having a natural beginning and end, as any good script should have. Remember a demo is used to show off your voice; it doesn't have to be a really swish, produced piece.

4.6   I need help making my demo. Who do I go to?

If you've decided that you need some guidance when creating your first demo, there are a number of reputable companies that can assist you. You may still want to source your own scripts if you want to be unique, or just take their guidance and use their stock scripts.

Most showreel production companies are based in London and charges will be around £200–£400. For these prices you can get anywhere between a couple of hours to a full day in the studio. To make the most of your studio time, practise and perfect your style at home first, before you book yourself onto one of these sessions.

You'll usually come away with at least separate commercial and narrative demos of about 90 seconds each. They'll be put on a CD for you ready for duplicating and probably in MP3 format for you to email/upload.

Some showreel production companies will also help you to record just one or two extra samples to freshen up an existing showreel, or if you have your own recordings they can edit them into a new or existing reel.

Some of our voices have used the following companies:
   Hot Reels www.hotreels.co.uk
   Silver Tongued Productions www.silver-tongued.co.uk
   The Showreel www.theshowreel.com
   Vox Training www.voxtraining.com

4.7 How can I avoid the most common demo "mistakes"?

We've received and reviewed thousands of voiceover demos and these are a few issues often highlighted:

- Poor studio or microphone sound.

- Over-emphasis on acting and audio book samples.

- No standard corporate narration.

- Too much focus on characters and accents when the voice artist isn't very good at them.

- No dry studio sample (no music, SFX or compression).

- Samples which aren't from their regular studio.

- Singing demos.

- Demos with dated audio such as clips more than two years old.

- Demos which mention brand names but weren't genuine recordings.

- Commercial radio reads spoken too slowly (generally real commercials pack as much into their 30 seconds as possible).

- Trying to sound like a stereotypical voiceover.

- No variation in mood so the samples blend into one and don't stand out.

- Random clips presenting a radio show.

- Copying well known adverts that they've seen on the TV.

- Over-production of music/sounds/whooshes/bangs which detract from the voice.

- Bad microphone technique with popping and peaking.

Chapter 5

Equipment and Studio Sound

5.1   How much does it cost to hire a studio?

At the expensive end, a dedicated voiceover or post-production studio in central London usually costs between £100–£250 per hour. This quality of studio will generally be used if a client needs to be present and they want to create a good impression.

If you shop around, you can probably make savings if you only require a simple functional broadcast quality studio, without all the frills.

If you're on a budget you can save money but maintain quality by using a studio that's not in central London and/or considering a studio that is geared towards recording music. Music studios are often a lot cheaper than voice studios but it's crucial to check they've got a good vocal microphone and a booth. It's unlikely that a music studio will have ISDN facilities but they should be able to save your recordings or email them to your client on your behalf. Please see the next question for help finding a reliable studio.

5.2 How do I find a good external studio?

If you're based in a city where there are lots of studios then word of mouth is probably your best method of finding a reliable studio.

Factors to look at include:

- Hourly rate.
- Can you hire for less than an hour (15/30 min slots) for smaller jobs?
- ISDN capabilities and costs involved.
- Do they have a dedicated vocal booth?
- Do they have a good vocal microphone (e.g. Neumann TLM103/49/193/U87)?
- Are they experienced in recording the spoken voice as opposed to music?
- Will they help you engineer (record) the session?
- How available are the studios for short notice jobs?
- Travel costs and time for you to get to the studio.
- Other listen-in capabilities such as phone patch/Skype/Source Connect.
- Any hidden charges for delivery of your audio etc.?

It's helpful to ask for a copy of a voice recording that they've made recently, so you or the client can gauge quality. Ensure it's a dry sample (no background music/SFX and no processing on the voice).

5.3   What studio equipment will I need?

The equipment you may need in your studio (or indeed see in an external studio) includes:

- XLR mic – Most professional microphones have an XLR connector, which is a large round three-pin connector.

- XLR to USB gadget – For simpler studio setups, some voices will connect their microphone direct to their computers. This usually allows them to make their own recordings and the setup is much simpler. However there are limitations and traditional pieces of studio equipment may not be usable.

- Pop shield – This helps remove "plosives" from your speech, also sometimes called a "popper stopper". Most microphones will need one of these for vocal work.

- Microphone amp (phantom power) – Most professional microphones require power which is normally sent down the XLR cable. Your mic will plug into a pre-amp, or mic amp, and this will amplify the mic signal and also provide power if necessary. A Mic amp is usually close to the microphone as a long cable leading to a pre-amp will tend to pick up background noise and reduce audio quality.

- Headphones – A good pair of headphones is essential; DT100s are very popular and almost the industry standard.

- Headphone amp – A headphone amp is often used if more than one pair of headphones is required. So if you had a studio which was used for double headers, for example, each voice would require their own pair of headphones.

- Mixing desk – A mixing desk is basically used for connecting everything together and controlling the input and output levels. It's essential to allow you to do certain things like connecting your TBU. For larger setups you may find a small mixing desk in the booth with the mic (for example to control sending the microphone signal to ISDN or computer), and a larger mixing desk outside the booth which connects the other pieces of equipment.

- Good software – Many software options will allow you to record your voiceovers, but some offer additional functionality which can make your life simpler or your recordings better (for example removing noise or normalising the audio). Some voice artists will lightly process their audio before delivering, if they think the end client would appreciate this, athough many producers prefer the audio without processing. We find a lot of voice artists use Adobe Audition, but check out demo versions of products before you purchase, and buy one you feel comfortable with.

- ISDN lines and codec/box – An ISDN codec will allow you to link up to other studios for "live" sessions.

- Computer/soundcard – If you are making your own recordings you'll need a computer and a good soundcard to ensure professional sound quality. An exception may be if you are being recorded by a different studio via an ISDN link.

- TBU – A TBU, or Telephone Balance Unit, allows a telephone line to be linked to your mixing desk. Sometimes also called a "Telephone hybrid", it allows someone to listen in on your recording – which is common when the end client wants to give live feedback, but does not have access to or does not want the cost of using an ISDN studio. Please see Question 5.10 "How can I set up a phone-patch facility?".

- Lighting – Good lighting to ensure you can read the script. Some bulbs make a noise, so beware of this, plus it's best to choose energy saving bulbs which produce less heat.

- Fax/virtual fax – Although email is used more, some companies still like to fax their scripts. If you do not send faxes often, we'd recommend trying a "virtual fax", whereby you are given a fax number and any received faxes are emailed to you. Have a look at suppliers like www.voiptalk.org.

- Noise gate – Some mic pre-amps will include a noise gate feature, or you can get a separate box for this. A noise gate allows you to configure a volume where the box will cut all audio. It means if you stop speaking, the noise gate kicks in and the background noise is cut.

- De-esser – Again this may be a separate box or included in a microphone amp. It will have settings which will remove sibilance (see Glossary) from an audio signal. If you are using ISDN for live recordings this is useful to remove the sibilance "on the fly". Alternatively sibilance can often be removed after recording using software.

- Talkback – Talkback is used in studios where an engineer will help make recordings. It allows the engineer in the studio to talk to the voiceover who is sitting in the booth. The engineer will have a basic microphone and this will feed into the main mixing desk. The engineer can then control whether the voice artist can hear him/her speak.

- Associated cabling – With each piece of equipment you'll usually find there is an associated vital lead required. In a studio situation it's normally an XLR to XLR lead but others will be required.

For more information try searching online for these terms:
  recording studio equipment
  home recording studio

5.4   What is the best microphone to use for voiceover work?

There are two types of microphone – condenser and dynamic. Dynamic microphones are mainly designed for a live environment. For voiceover work in a studio, you'll want to use a large diaphragm microphone, which is a type of condenser microphone.

A popular choice is the Neumann TLM 103 as it is a high quality, yet relatively affordable, mic costing around £800. There are others in the Neumann range to consider such as the TLM 49, TLM 193 and U87. Although Neumann is a favourite amongst voiceovers we've also received great quality recordings made using AKG, Audio Technica and Shure microphones.

5.5   How do I configure my microphone? (patterns)

Many condenser microphones have a setting for different "patterns". These patterns dictate how the microphone picks up sound. If your microphone has such a setting, the most appropriate for voiceover work is generally the "cardioid" pattern which is usually indicated by a heart shaped symbol. This pattern will block sound from the rear of the microphone, giving more emphasis to the front and the sides.

Some microphones can rotate over time and with a muff/pop shield this can go unnoticed. Due to the pattern it's important to regularly check that the microphone is pointing towards you.

You may notice other patterns such as "bidirectional", mainly used for interview situations with a person either side of the microphone, and "omni directional", which picks up sound from all directions and is used for recording ambient sounds.

If your microphone has additional settings, identify the best setting using trial and error, listening back to your recordings with a good pair of headphones and choosing the best setting for your environment.

5.6   What is a suitable space for my voice booth?

Firstly you need a physical space to locate your booth; choose somewhere as small as possible. As long as you can fit in there with a chair and small desk, the smallest space will be easiest to sound condition. The ideal room size would be around 4 feet x 5 feet. Avoiding a completely square room is better for the acoustics. Bear in mind you may have to add 6 inches or more for soundproofing materials. Some voiceover artists have started out using their under stairs cupboard or walk-in wardrobe. Obviously think about noises from above/below and find a quiet spot away from traffic noise... or kids!

If you are using a larger room, you are likely to want to have a standalone structure within this, to use as your booth. Something the size of a small shed could be ideal.

5.7 What is the difference between sound conditioning and soundproofing?

A good studio should be both sound conditioned and soundproof.

Soundproofing is making sure noises outside of the booth are not picked up by the microphone. Soundproofing is obtained by having thick insulation in the studio walling.

Sound conditioning ensures that when you speak within the booth, there is no reverberation. Sound conditioning is more difficult and involves the use of acoustic wall panels and sometimes shaping the booth so that audio doesn't reflect back towards the microphone.

5.8   What's   the   cheapest   way   to   create   a soundproof studio?

There is no real substitute for a properly constructed and soundproof booth, using all the professional material and panels that are available. However this can cost thousands of pounds. If you are starting out recording at home, you may be able to make an effective recording area which is 90% effective.

You will see products that claim to create mobile studios or reflector devices to combat reverb, but our experience shows these are not high enough quality to be used as a permanent solution.

Once you've found a space for your booth, ensure it is equipped with light and power. It's best if your computer tower/base unit is situated outside of the recording area to prevent fan noise. The first step is to soundproof the walls and cover any windows. A cheap way of doing this is to create an insulated wall using two-by-two wood, rock wool (loft insulation) and plasterboard. It's good to create a fake floor using high density loft boarding and ensuring the sides of the floor do not touch the walls, to prevent vibrations passing onto the floor. Once this has been done, choose a location for the microphone and if the room is "off square" place the microphone on the shortest wall as this can help prevent sound reflections. Cover the walls inside the booth with soft furnishings, ideally sound panelling but if this is too expensive use thick, dense materials. Cover the floor with a thick rug. Ensure the area directly behind the microphone, i.e. the wall facing you as you speak, has a good amount of soft furnishings. You will sense a good soundproof environment as it will sound "dead" when you speak.

5.9   What's involved in setting up an ISDN facility?

In the voiceover world ISDN allows two studios to perform a "live link up" with high quality sound, so a remote producer can direct and record your voice from their own studio which may be anywhere in the world.

A regular phone line is generally an analogue line but for ISDN you need two digital lines (channels). When a voice artist has ISDN it means they have rented an ISDN line and have an ISDN codec box. The codec box is connected to the line and will convert audio to a digital signal and vice versa.

So you will need a single ISDN line which consists of two digital channels. On the technical side, each channel is 64 Kbps, so you have 128 Kbps data speed.

When you try to rent an ISDN line some telecoms companies may assume you are trying to connect to the internet, and may advise you to get broadband. Broadband is not an alternative to ISDN for voiceovers. The difference is, ISDN is point-to-point which means once you are connected to the other studio you have exclusive use of the full 128 Kbps speed. Broadband just lets you connect to the internet and when you connect to another internet user your speed/bandwidth is not guaranteed and so isn't as reliable as ISDN.

You should purchase an ISDN line through your local telecoms company. For BT, this tends to be called "2e". This may cost around £100 per quarter. You may hear some voices talk about a legacy BT product called "Home Highway". This was cheaper than "2e" as it was marketed for internet access when broadband was not as widespread as it is now – but this service is no longer on offer.

Once you have an ISDN line, you will need an ISDN codec box to allow you to connect to other ISDN producers/studios. There are many codec boxes available for purchase and you can choose between a full hardware solution (a rack mounted box), a computer based solution such as ISYS PRO or indeed a software based solution such as AudioTx.

Not all ISDN codecs speak the same language, so you should check that the one you buy is common for your market.

In the UK, using two channels and an Mpeg 2 protocol is the most common. It will offer a quality audio transfer, adequate for most uses.

An old favourite is the Musicam CDQ Prima codec box, which you may be able to find second hand for around £1,000. These boxes tend to run and run and many have been in operation for 10 to 20 years. They can be a little daunting, but once set up they are easy to operate.

As mentioned briefly above, you can also get PC based ISDN systems such as ISYS PRO and AudioTx communicator. These can be more cost effective, and easier to use. Some can automatically detect the incoming ISDN protocol and adapt as necessary, which means less messing about adjusting the settings. You'll need to purchase and maintain a computer, ISDN card and high quality soundcard. It would be recommended that you dedicate the computer solely for this purpose and not treat it as a general use computer.

Once you are set up with ISDN and your codec, make a test connection to another studio and make sure that your codec is "framing". Basically when your two channels have successfully connected and audio can flow both ways, the call is said to have "framed". It means that both ISDN codecs have had a little chat and are now sending audio to each other.

ISDN lines are not perfect, however, and ISDN dropouts can occasionally occur. This is like a CD skipping where some of the data is lost in transit. You shouldn't need to worry as the producer on the other end should spot any dropouts and get you to repeat if required.

It's etiquette for a producer to call into your ISDN, but if you do make ISDN calls, remember it will cost twice as much as a normal call as you will be using two channels simultaneously.

For more information try searching online for these terms:
  Musicam CDQ prima
  ISDN2e lines
  ISDN audio codec
  AudioTx

5.10   How can I set up a phone-patch facility?

A phone patch allows somebody to listen in to a recording in your studio via standard telephone. It can be beneficial to clients who want to listen in and give input on style or pronunciations. You will still need to record and deliver your own recordings, as they will only hear telephone quality audio.

Setting up a phone patch can be done in a number of ways:

• Use your ISDN codec. Some codecs (usually the PC based ones) may switch into analogue mode and will automatically link in a standard call.

• Ad hoc (amateur way). Get a cordless phone and just take it into the booth with you. Easy and cheap but not very professional, plus you might not be able to mute a traditional phone so client noises could be picked up by your microphone.

• Link–in a PC to your mixing desk which is running VOIP software (Voice Over IP), such as Skype or a SIP softphone (e.g. ExpressTalk or similar). Skype allows companies throughout the world to listen in at low cost and is easier to set up than SIP. Some users find SIP more reliable than Skype but this varies so it's best to decide by trial and error. Both would allow you to have a dedicated phone number for your patch without requiring a physical phone line.

• Link a TBU box into your studio, sometimes called a "Telephone hybrid". These can be quite costly and will tend to link into a traditional analogue line. As you are using a traditional analogue line you can overcome most of the reliability problems that a VOIP solution may have.

More info about bullet 3, above:

There are free Skype or SIP softphones obtainable from websites like www.download.com or www.skype.com. Skype will allow a "Skype in" number to be rented, which means you can give clients a telephone number to call in for session monitoring.

For a SIP account, see a provider like VOIPtalk http://www.voiptalk.org.

For SIP accounts and a SIP softphone, you may need to change router settings for it to be able to receive and send calls properly. Be advised by looking at the help on the particular provider/softphone websites.

For Skype, generally it can be installed and it will work without making router changes.

Once the software is installed, check whether you need to change the sound input and output settings, so that they can hear you and you can hear them, without them being recorded. It's probably beneficial to have a separate mixing desk in the booth, even if it's a small one. This will allow you to ensure all the INs and OUTs are being passed to the right places and that levels can be changed quickly if required.

For more information try searching online for these terms:
Skype
SIP softphone
SIP account
telephone hybrid
Express Talk
VOIPtalk
download.com

5.11   I've been told that my audio has reverb. What do I do?

Reverb is caused by audio bouncing off the walls, ceiling and floor, then back into the microphone. This can cause a problem for producers as it's almost impossible to remove or clean up in post production. To combat reverb, ensure your walls, ceiling and floor are covered in a soft, dense material. If you have soundproof panels and are still getting reverb, check there is no hard surface, such as a window or desk, which could be causing an audio reflection. Experiment using cushions and other soft furnishings that absorb sound. If you can't hear the problem yourself, check you are listening back to your recordings using professional headphones.

5.12 How do I know whether there's background noise on my recording?

On the wave below you can see clear peaks of speech. Between these, you'd ideally see nothing at all; however on this recording you can see a thin, roughly flat line of recorded sound. This sound may have been caused by bad wiring or something in the studio making a consistent low noise, such as a computer fan.

If you can see and hear irregular background sounds (rather than a background hum), they're likely to be coming from something else such as jewellery you're wearing or outside noises breaking through your studio soundproofing.

It's a nice idea to record your raw studio sound with no speech to check the ambient noise level and resolve any issues you find.

As mentioned earlier, a noise gate will prevent low volume noises, such as clothing rustle, from being recorded as it will only open the channel when louder noises, such as your voice, are registered in the microphone.

The image below shows how a low volume noise would register when the noise gate is switched off and then subsequently switched on (1). The audio recorded with the noise gate on is much "cleaner".

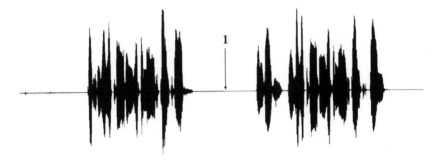

However using a noise gate isn't a solution to a bad studio sound. Always look to improve your soundproofing first and use a noise gate as the icing on the cake.

Chapter 6

Recording Yourself – Technical Considerations

6.1   What's expected when I deliver voiceover recordings?

If you are asked to record yourself, it is common practice to deliver your recording:

- Free of errors (out-takes removed) and proofed to make sure it matches the script.

- With no background noise or reverberation.

- With alternative takes where a pronunciation or direction is unclear.

- With multiple takes of the full script if the script is small (less than a page). Ensure you have enough variation between each take.

- In an uncompressed format if requested (WAV or AIFF).

- De-breathed where intrusive breaths appear between sentences (but not mid sentence).

If the client is unhappy with the audio or style of delivery, a voice artist would normally be expected to re-record without additional expense. The exception would be if the script has been changed. It's therefore your responsibility to check the script prior to recording and ask the clients any questions concerning pronunciations and style. Also if it's a long script we recommend recording a short sample so your client can approve the style. This reduces the risk of having to re-record the full script.

Here are a few extra things that you or a producer may do:

- Removal of "mouth noises" – Any mouth noises or paper rustles between sentences can be stripped out leaving a clean recording. If these noises form part of a word then they're difficult to remove and it's easier to re-record the whole sentence.

- De-essing – It's sometimes possible to remove sibilance on intrusive "esss" noises, but consider using equipment to remove sibilance during recording if you find you have a problem with it.

- Dynamics processing/compression – This often levels the audio, reducing the volume of loud parts and boosting quiet parts. The resulting audio often sounds punchier and more "dynamic".

- Edit the audio into multiple files.

- Provide the audio in a specialist format such as encoding used in the telecoms industry.

- Provide the audio mixed with music.

- Time stretch – This is best avoided but can help in situations where timing is an issue.

- Add reverb – Reverb may sometimes be added to lift your voice above background music or to add ambience.

- Clever editing to use the best parts of multiple takes and produce a new "perfect take".

6.2   What do my recordings look like?

It's important to be familiar with the visual representation of your recorded audio.

When opening your recording in a software package, you're likely to see it displayed similar to the image below.

In simple terms, think of it as a graph of level/volume (1) as time (2) progresses.

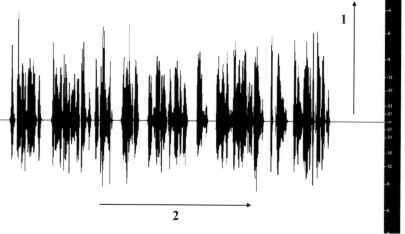

On most audio programs you can zoom into this visual representation to an increasing degree.

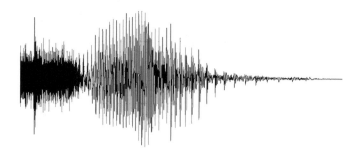

6.3   How do I know whether my recording level is correct?

We would advise recording with your levels peaking between –8dB and –4dB.

If the recording volume is too quiet, your recording will fill very little of the screen and may be displayed like this.

Although you can amplify a quiet recording, you'll affect the whole recording including any background noise. It means the resulting audio may sound dirty or hissy.

At the other end of the spectrum, if your recording level is too loud your wave will overspill and may look like this.

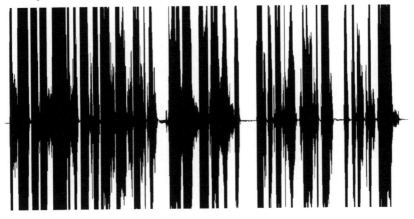

Recording with the levels too loud can cause distortion and you can never recover the "lost" peaks which have overspilled. It's therefore very important that you record at the correct level, otherwise it may be necessary to re-record the full script.

6.4   Why should I record multiple takes of the intro and outro of a script?

An intro needs to attract attention and gain the interest of the listener. First impressions are important, so if the client is happy with the intro, they're much more likely to approve the whole recording.

The outro of a script is generally the call to action or the conclusion and is arguably equally important as the intro.

A good tip is to re-record the intro of the script at the end of the session when you're into the swing of things. You can then edit this back into the start.

6.5   How do I cut out my mistakes?

The first step in removing your errors is to ensure they can be easily identified when you edit, so you can efficiently find the mistakes by sight.

Most voices will record the whole script in one go and remove errors and tidy up the recording afterwards.

If you have access to your keyboard in the booth, some programs will allow you to insert an edit point or marker whilst you're recording by pressing a key. This places a vertical line which you can see when you later view the recording and you can quickly identify where the problems are.

In this example, the sentence starts (1) but the voiceover artist made a mistake. The recording continues and a marker is added by the voiceover artist (2) to indicate that they are beginning the sentence again (3).

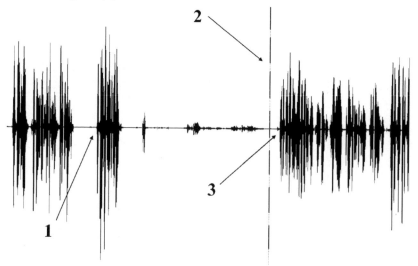

If you are unable to insert a marker as described, why not just pause? You can then spot the quiet parts and therefore indentify the mistakes. Other voices have been known to clap, or have a whistle, clicker etc.: something which can be identified easily when viewing the recording.

Cutting out mistakes is almost as simple as deleting text in a word processor. In most audio programs you just select the region you want to delete and press the "Delete" key.

You'll want to listen back to the recording in those areas to check you are deleting the correct region!

In the next image, you will see the voiceover artist has selected the area to be deleted. It's common to identify the start of the "good" sentence first, and then click and drag back to highlight the sentence containing the mistake.

Ensure you maintain the natural space or breath so that it doesn't sound like an obvious edit.

See below, the error is selected (1) ready to delete.

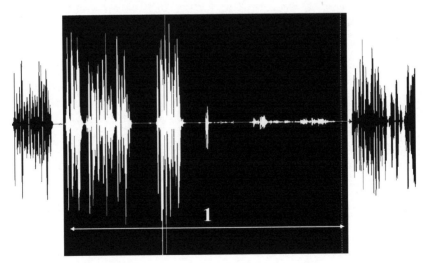

After you have edited out the mistakes, save to a new file, keeping a backup of the original recording in case you chopped out something important by accident!

When recording yourself, it's wise to listen back and check your accuracy prior to delivery.

6.6   What software package should I choose?

Most audio software packages allow simple recording, editing and saving which will probably be adequate for you when starting out.

A basic free option is a program called "Audacity" which can be obtained from an official download site such as www.download.com.

Ensure the program you choose supports at least the following:

- Recording from external sources/sound card.

- Saving to multiple formats including WAV, AIFF, MP3.

- Support for 44.1kHz or 48kHz bit rates.

- High quality MP3 support including 128Kbps mono or higher.

- Simple editing to allow you to cut out errors.

If you're dealing directly with an end client and providing editing services or making your own productions, you may want to consider a package with more features. Pro Tools and Adobe Audition (previously known as Cool Edit Pro) seem to have become the industry standard. They also allow additional plug-ins to further expand the capabilities.

6.7   How do I de-breath my recordings?

On the image below you can see a clear indication of loud breath noises. You can recognise these as the smaller diamond/triangle shapes appearing between the peaks of speech.

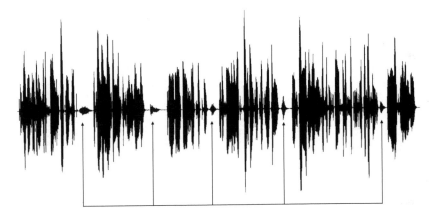

Not everybody's breath noises look the same but after a couple of recordings it's really easy to recognise your own. Breath noises can be removed by highlighting them and silencing them using your audio software. If your producer has not requested de-breathed audio you probably don't need to worry about this at all, but if you're delivering to an end client it's something to consider. It's also worth noting that de-breathing can be time consuming.

Some voices will silence just the breaths in between sentences, and leave breaths that occur within sentences so that the recording sounds natural. Others have almost silent or generally quiet breaths, and they may not appear to be intrusive. We know voices who have naturally loud breaths and will employ techniques such as turning slightly away from the microphone as they breathe, so that they don't register loudly on the recording.

6.8   What are mouth noises?

Mouth noises are not usually attractive noises! Commonly caused by a dry mouth, they're the sound of your mouth parts sticking together when you talk – tongue, cheek, soft palette. You can identify them below as the very small spikes appearing between the obvious larger sections of speech.

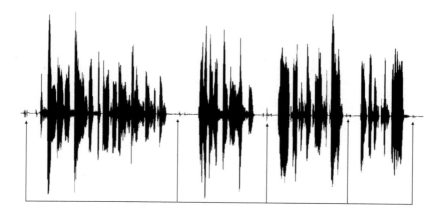

Similar to de-breathing, the best way to remove these would be to highlight and silence them using your audio software. If you find these occur very often, you could be suffering from a dry mouth. A simple sip of water occasionally throughout your recording session may help resolve it. Some voices also find sugar-free gum and mints (especially those with Xylitol) help the mouth produce saliva.

6.9   What does popping look like on my recording?

On the image below you can see the difference between regular speech and a "pop". The rush of breath causes the microphone to register a sudden distorted spike in the wave. Midway through the wave below you can see a word which has "popped" followed by three further popping noises.

They're normally easy enough to hear but it's helpful if you can visually identify them too. If you do find you have words popping, it's best to re-record rather than faff with editing/processing.

If you really want to attempt to remove a pop on a recording, try filtering out the bass from that small section or reducing the volume of the pop.

6.10   What does a compressed recording look like?

In this question we do not mean data compression that occurs when saving as an MP3 file, we mean audio compression or any form of audio processing which "flattens" a recording.

Compression boosts the smaller peaks of the wave and reduces the larger peaks. Essentially it will bring the two volume extremities closer together which is clear to see in the following images.

It's not something you can reverse and many producers like to apply it themselves. If you do apply compression to your audio, always keep the original unprocessed file as a backup as it may be required in the future.

Some voiceover artists will apply a light amount of processing to remove irregular peaks and at the same time boost quieter parts.

Look at the following three images of the same recording. The first is the raw recording, with no compression.

In the next image, a medium degree of compression has been applied which does not cause the recording to "flat line".

And in the final image, the recording is strongly compressed. This recording will sound punchier and richer, but has lost subtleness and some definition.

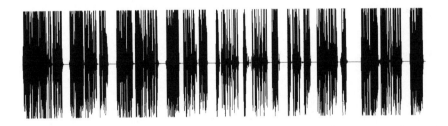

Many audio software programs will have compression presets or let you store your own, so play about and find which suits your voice best. You may choose to apply different processing for different clients or styles, for example your "movie trailer" preset. Do ensure you keep good records so you can deliver your audio in a consistent manner. Some voices deliver compressed and raw versions so the client can choose which they prefer.

6.11   How do I deliver large audio files?

Delivering large recordings by email can be slightly problematic, especially if your client wants WAV files. Large audio files may bounce, or worse, clog up a producer's inbox if they're not expecting them. Alternative methods of delivery would be to use FTP (see the next question for more info); using a delivery service such as www.yousendit.com which is a simpler way of delivering your audio electronically; or talking to your client and checking whether you can deliver the recording encoded as an MP3 file.

6.12   What is FTP and how can I use it?

FTP stands for file transfer protocol and is a method of transferring files from one computer to another via the internet. It's ideally suited for large files such as audio recordings that are sometimes impractical to email. A client may provide you with FTP logon details, which is basically the information you need to connect to their computer. In this situation, you can enter this into your FTP software, connect to their computer and drag and drop your recordings.

In addition, it may also be worth considering buying yourself some FTP space, so that you can deliver your audio by uploading it to your own space and giving your clients the logon information.

You can use Windows Explorer (My Computer) for FTP transfers, but it's quite basic and specially designed FTP programs may offer additional features.

If you find FTP complicated, you may find a system like www.yousendit.com is easier to use.

For more information try searching online for these terms:
  Download.com
  FTP software
  FTP space
  Yousendit
  Mailbigfile

6.13   What options should I select when creating MP3 files?

When you create an MP3 file, there are various options which affect the quality and the size of the resulting file. A standard in the voiceover world is to use 16-bit resolution, 128Kbps mono encoding. Basically the higher the Kbps, the higher the quality. Any less than 128Kbps would probably not be sufficiently high quality.

Bear in mind that most microphones are mono so recording in stereo is of no benefit and will merely double the file size. A 128Kbps stereo MP3 is about the same quality as a 64Kbps mono MP3 and therefore not sufficiently high quality.

6.14   Do I use 44.1kHz or 48kHz?

This refers to the sampling rate used when the audio is recorded. As a general rule, clients who work heavily in telecoms or film making would prefer 48kHz, whereas if the audio is destined for a website or PC use, clients generally prefer 44.1kHz.

It's better to set this prior to recording although you can convert between the two with slight degradation in quality. At the end of the day, this is the client's preference and it's best just to mention before recording what your sampling rate is in case they have any issues.

If a client complains that they can't play your audio once delivered and you've recorded at 48kHz, it may be preferable to downsample to 44.1kHz and re-deliver (downsampling can be done using most audio editing programs).

6.15   What are the common audio formats?

For uncompressed audio, use WAV for PC and WAV or AIFF for Mac. For compressed audio, MP3 is the most common format and suitable for both PC and Mac.

If a client is a telecoms supplier, they may ask for recordings in a specialist format e.g. μ-law, GSM. This is not something a voiceover artist would be expected to do, as the client should have a process to take care of this. If this isn't the case, a production company should be able to help them for a small fee.

6.16   Do I charge to tidy my own recordings?

You should factor in the time it takes you to clean your recordings (and any extras such as de-breathing) in your initial quote. However if it takes you an hour to tidy your recording you can't justify charging another hour session fee. Your fee should reflect the wage of an audio editor which may be around £10 an hour. If you find this job to be time consuming, have a look at our tips earlier in this chapter. If you still can't get your head around it you should consider paying someone else to tidy your audio. It's never acceptable to deliver a bad recording.

Chapter 7

Script Preparation

7.1   Whose responsibility is it to ensure the pronunciations are correct?

In nearly all cases it is your responsibility to ensure that pronunciations are correct. If you're unsure or it's ambiguous, it is advisable to check prior to recording or record alternative takes, which is feasible if the word occurs only a few times. As with all script queries, try to get into the habit of checking through a script as soon as you get confirmation to record, rather than leaving it until the session, as the client may be unavailable to confirm. Also, check how acronyms and telephone numbers should be spoken, and whether they prefer "slash" or "forward slash", "hyphen" or "dash" in web addresses.

If the worst happens and the pronunciation issue is not picked up until after delivery, it's good etiquette to offer a free re-record of that particular sentence or paragraph.

Invest in a pronunciation dictionary to help yourself. A good online resource is http://dictionary.cambridge.org/ which can also offer tips on phonetics, diphthongs and other dictionary symbols. You can now test your dictionary as you go to look up what a "diphthong" is!

With tricky names or foreign place names, ask the client to leave the pronunciation in a voicemail or record a guide track using a cheap desktop microphone.

If you're really stuck and the client isn't available, try searching on YouTube or search the web for the problem word and include "pronounced"; for example "Totnes pronounced" or "Totnes is pronounced".

7.2 How do I mark up a script?

Prior to the session, it's an excellent idea to read through and mark up your script. Don't assume that the person who wrote the script will be a competent copywriter. Therefore, as you read through, add commas for pausing and quote marks for words you want to group into phrases (see examples below).

Before you begin, check the style that the client wants as this may affect your marking up. For example do they want you to naturally contract words like "it is" to "it's"? A complicated tutorial narration may require more pauses, so that it's easier for the listener to follow.

Sometimes you'll need to pause for breath which you can indicate by a slash (/) between words. Underline or highlight words you think it would be best to stress.

Write pronunciations for acronyms/unusual words in the margins and re-read your script after you've marked it up. You may wish to print your scripts with some line spacing to allow you to fit in extra marks during the recording session.

During the session you may want to indicate an upward or downward inflection on the script. It's common to use an upward or downward pointing arrow or accent over that particular word. Some voiceovers will add smiley faces or other symbols to prompt them to change style, such as a smiley end to a script.

Please see the example script on the next page.

Announcer. Mature, steady paced but vulnerable at first. Brightens up for second half.

"It wasn't until I had a fall and broke my hip that I realised I'm not getting any younger.

Time goes past so quickly and before you know it old age is creeping up on you and it's then you realise that you haven't prepared for what happens to your possessions when you're not here anymore.

A friend gave me a phone number for "Barton Bull and Sallance" Solicitors and they were very friendly and helpful. Most importantly, to my surprise, they didn't cost the earth!

If you want peace of mind too Call them on 0880 8383 555 and tell them Margaret/Martin said hi."

7.3   How can I improve my sight reading?

Excellent sight reading is an essential skill for voiceover artists.

There are a few common problems and below are some tips to combat these.

1)   Regressing – This is automatically reading back words that you've already read. To combat this you should practise reading scripts at a fast pace and using your finger to guide as you go along. This will keep the focus moving forwards on the script. Do this practice once a day until the issue eases.

2)   Comprehension – Reading unfamiliar words can slow your sight reading. There's a simple solution to this but it does involve practice. Read new literature frequently and discipline yourself to keep up the habit.

3)   Widen your eye-span – At school we're taught to read slowly and carefully take in one word at a time. This habit continues but can make the sentence sound stilted. Try to read blocks of words such as four or five at a time then move your focus to the next group of words rather than individually. You'll find you'll be able to comprehend the flow of the sentence earlier, and your speech will convey your understanding.

7.4   What do I do if my script arrives in an awkward format?

Your scripts can arrive in all sorts of formats such as PDF, PowerPoint, Excel, JPEG, fax and so on, but it's perfectly valid to ask for something more familiar, like a Word document, that you find easier to format. It's advisable to format scripts to a standard setting, such as Arial font, size 11, double line spaced. This helps you gauge the script size to provide consistent quotes, plus sight reading a script in a familiar font will be easier.

Some Microsoft Word scripts will have "comments" and "track changes" left in which can obscure the text. If these aren't offering guidance for you, you can remove them by selecting "accept all changes in document" and "delete all comments in document".

7.5   How do I match my timings to a video?

If your voice recording will be used on a video and the visuals have already been made, then you may be asked to record to time. Clarify to what degree, which may be one of the following:

- Lip-synching – You need to match your sentences in time with the person on screen. For this you'll need a professional studio with lip-synching facilities unless you have a screen with the relevant software/equipment in your home studio. This is most commonly used when dubbing from another language.

- Hit certain words at specific times – You can do this from home if you have access to a screen in your studio, such as a laptop that you can take in the booth with you. It's most commonly used for tutorial narrations when the script will say "click here for..." and you'll need to speak at the same time as the cursor clicks a button.

- Recording sentences and short paragraphs to time – If the visuals have been finalised prior to the voice recording you'll need to match the lengths of your sentences with those annotated on your script (usually in a separate "timings" column). If the client doesn't provide the timings, you may need to preview the video/guide track and add the timings yourself.

The best results are obtained if the client can tweak the visuals to match a voiceover recording. This means the voiceover can be recorded at a consistent, natural pace rather than varying the speed.

Chapter 8

Voice Delivery and Technique

8.1   Can I learn character voices?

Character voices and impressions can be tough to crack, so who better to tell you about this than Guy Harris (www.voiceoverguy.co.uk). Guy is an established character voiceover and here are a few tips from the man himself:

Can Anyone Do Characters/Impressions? Yeah, anyone can do them! You always hear the line, "My mate does a great Del Boy".

Lots of people can imitate famous voices but the real skill lies in learning how a character speaks when they are not delivering the line they are most famous for. I know people who can say "I don't believe it!" and sound like Victor Meldrew. But ask them to say something else and they struggle. The reason being they have spent so long perfecting the catchphrase, they have neglected to learn how Victor speaks the rest of the time.

YouTube is full of videos of "100 characters in two minutes". Amazing impressions... (for most) of catchphrases. Now this isn't me having a pop at these people at all, no way. I love watching them, they are very talented indeed and it's fantastic entertainment along with a nice party piece.

However when it comes to imitating people or performing as a character professionally like the awesome Jon Culshaw or Alistair McGowan, you have to be able to say more than "Just like that" or "My name is Michael Caine". These guys study the characters for hours on end, working out every inflection and characteristic of the voice.

Personally I try to imagine I am the character and this helps me a lot. When I become Johnny Vegas I actually believe I am stood in a bar with a pint of Guinness and a stuffed monkey sat next to me. When I do Alan Partridge I see myself stood in a blazer and slacks, Lynn with me and my giant dinner plate in the hand before I try to speak like him.

It might sound odd, but it does help if you try to put yourself in the shoes of the person you are imitating.

Here is a great thing about characters and a true story. When I was younger I had my first real snog with a girl after I impressed her with a barrage of characters on a bus into town. Mmmm, maybe she did it to shut me up???

Random Characters...

So, you get asked by a producer to play a horse, a dog, a mafia mobster or a tiny mouse.

Can you play these? Absolutely. How?

Practise! That's all there is to it. Try to copy things around you. People, noises, animals, any unusual sounds you hear too. Now I know this might sound odd, but as a kid I used to imitate my teachers, I used to make unusual noises, copy silly sounds I would hear on TV, but hey, it's given me a great career and I am so glad of the day that I stood up at the front of class and pretended to be our maths teacher for 15 minutes, when he was late. It was also worth the telling off that I got when he walked in whilst I was midway through ranting like he used to!

Where to Practise?

The car! What a great place to perfect a voice! There you are on your own in your semi soundproof 70mph booth. Who cares what the guy next to you thinks of your mouth contorting into all shapes as you try to find a voice to sound like an angry dog for your next job???

When I am driving, I look at people next to me in stationary traffic and try to imagine how they might sound. Yeah I know, I need to get out more.

As a teenager I always wanted to be able to talk like Don LaFontaine, the late great movie trailer guy who sadly passed away in 2008. I committed to working on his style and over the years of practising and reaching deeper and deeper into my vocal range I managed to achieve a pretty good impression. Not only that, but the style was picked up on and I got genuine TV commercials to advertise movies which has been a huge dream come true and something that wouldn't have happened without the commitment to learn Don's style. Check out www.movietrailerguy.co.uk.

Yes, some people find changing voices easy, and for some it's a little harder, but in my experience it's lack of confidence that holds them back. If you want to do this, use every opportunity to perfect your craft.

8.2   What's concatenation and how should it affect my voicing?

Concatenation is the joining of two or more voice clips to form a word or sentence. It is used where it would not be practical to record all the combinations of phrases such as on telephone systems and train platforms.

Take the following sentence: "Your call is number six in the queue and should be answered in about five minutes." This might actually be created by joining "your call is number" "six" "in the queue" "and should be answered in about" "five" "minutes". When voicing these types of scripts, you need to be careful with your intonation, so that when the sentence is created it sounds as natural as possible. A useful way to practise is to voice a full sentence, split it up and see whether you ended each section with an upward, flat or downward inflection and then repeat that inflection consistently for the other options. For example in "your call is number six in the queue" the inflection used for "six" should be used when speaking the options "one", "two" etc.

8.3   Can I learn accents?

Learning an accent so that you sound like a native requires skill and practice. You may find it's not worth the effort if there are already real native voiceovers covering this area. Never claim to have a native accent unless it really is genuine, as this can seriously damage your reputation.

If you've "neutralised" your voice but can recover your lost native accent you may find this is a unique selling point to consider.

Requests for accents will generally either be for spoof accents where accuracy is not too important, or for native accents which will need to be spot on. If you want to be active in the character voiceover market then it's definitely a good idea to learn a range of spoof accents.

To learn a new accent you need to have the skill to identify differences in dialects, so that you can pratise reproducing these until they sound natural. Assist yourself by marking up scripts where you need to adapt your voice or transcribe the entire script in phonetic form to guide your pronunciation. A good resource is the "Speech Accent Archive" which you can find online at http://accent.gmu.edu. It contains sample audio from hundreds of speakers around the world, allowing you to compare differences between dialects. Practice makes perfect. Have fun and spend time listening to recordings and teaching yourself.

8.4   What is "popping the mic" and how do I combat this?

Popping the mic is when the "p" or "sh" sounds cause distortion due to breath being exhaled directly into the microphone. These sounds are also called "plosives". Never deliver a recording with popping; it's a real no-no in the industry.

To combat popping, invest in a "pop filter" also called a "pop screen". Even with the screen you may still get popping, however. One technique would be to alter your direction when speaking plosives so that you're not facing the centre of the mic, but at a 45-degree angle instead. Just be careful not to go "off mic". Another technique that voiceover artists use is to half close their mouth when speaking the problem sounds. To practise this technique, put your hand in front of your mouth and monitor how much breath is exhaled when you say the problem sounds.

8.5   How do I change styles from corporate to commercial etc?

A professional voiceover artist must be versatile which may mean swapping from one style to another throughout the working day.

Have your common styles and previously recorded files to hand to refer to immediately before a session starts. This will help you switch into the correct style as it's not uncommon for corporate scripts to have pickups or additions.

Aim for a rough reading pace of 120–150 words per minute for corporate recordings and generally a pacier 150–180 words per minute or more for commercial scripts.

Proximity to your microphone affects the richness of your voice. For soft commercial and sincere corporate reads, close proximity is required. On a standard Neumann microphone you're talking around 5cm from the mic. For straight corporate scripts you could be around 10–15cm from the mic. Finally, for salesy commercials or formal announcements you may need to project your voice and aim for around 25cm distance between your mouth and the mic.

With any script remember to ask yourself "Who is my audience?" and "What role, mood and situation am I supposed to be in?".

Commercial radio

Commercials differ from corporate scripts in that commercials aim to grab the listener's attention in some way. Your tone will need to be "bouncier" which means your pitch will need to vary more than it ever would in standard speaking. For example most commercials require the "smile factor" when selling a product. Literally smile as you record and ooze enthusiasm. You'd be surprised at how much you need to exaggerate this as producers often request "extra cheese". However don't be fooled into thinking that commercial just means "salesy". There are so many ways to approach the text and get the desired response. Is the script emotive, tugging on the heart strings? Is it funny and grabbing the attention of the listener with a gag? Read through and decide the best way for you to tackle it. You can also ask the producer if you can hear the music which will be used. This will reflect the mood and could help you.

Commercial TV

Try to remember that with commercial TV scripts you'll have to adapt to a different style from commercial radio. With television you don't want to distract from what's happening on screen. You're merely directing their attention, not taking it. You don't need to focus on picture painting as the visuals are there already. Commercial TV scripts are normally written with a specific style of read in mind. You will have a director to help tease out the best take from you.

Commercial promos

With commercial promos the current trend is to "shock" the audience into wanting to watch. This can be describing a "killer bee" in a menacing fashion or remarking in delight at the chef on screen who has created the world's biggest pie. Your tone and inflections should be exaggerated to hook the audience.

Corporate recordings

As with many styles, with corporate scripts it can be useful to imagine your audience. If you're recording a train platform announcement, imagine a bustling crowd. Your words need to be clearly enunciated and precise. If you're voicing a health and safety video then imagine you are in a meeting room with a small group of people. You'll find your style will become friendly and informative. With some web videos you may need to be a little bit bouncier, as you are still aiming to grab an audience's attention.

There's a trend at the moment to have natural voices for corporate reads. Clients seem less taken by the typical formal approach; they want something a little more endearing and friendly.

Documentary recordings

Much like TV commercials, the visuals are in front of the viewer. Keep your voice in a comfortable range that won't be too distracting for the audience. You'll be directing their attention and guiding them through the story with nuggets of information. Before you record a documentary it would be well worth doing some research to see what type of voices the channel usually hires and the style they prefer. Keep your individuality and don't mimic another voice, but bear in mind the tone – it's obviously what the director likes.

> TIP:
> It's a common problem for voices to start a script loud, and then lose energy and volume over time.
> It's a bit like running a marathon... pace yourself and ensure that the energy you have at the start of the script continues right through to the end.

8.6   What are the different techniques to stress or highlight a word?

A script is about putting a message across and some words can be more important than others. You can emphasize these in many ways and it's good practice to vary the methods so that the listener remains interested.

Rehearse these techniques until they become second nature:

- Change pitch – higher or lower register

- Slight pause before and/or after the word

- Projection/volume

- Speed – generally by slowing down to emphasise

- Smile

Try this sentence a few times, picking out certain words with the techniques above:

"Come and visit us any weekday for your free and exclusive customer info pack."

8.7   How do I sound natural?

For aspiring artists one of the biggest skills to focus on is the ability to read a script in a natural manner that doesn't sound like it's being read. Read through the script a few times so that you understand the meaning of the content and you don't have to rely on your sight reading. It's important to feel relaxed with a script if you want to be believable. Try to visualise that you're speaking to a friend.

Practice makes perfect, so read more literature. Recognising words and groups of words easily before you speak them gives you more time to prepare how you say them. Over-emphasis or articulation and too much projection can lead to false reads; be aware and pull back on these areas if necessary.

Check that your pace isn't too uniform and ensure you use all the techniques available when stressing words (see the previous question) and don't just end each sentence with a downward inflection.

Unfortunately there isn't a simple solution but some voices will find it comes easier than others.

8.8 What is reading to time and how can I improve it?

Many commercial scripts will need to be spoken to very specific times. This is because each ad will have an allocated time slot, and scripts will be carefully written to maximise the use of this. In radio it's most common to have 30 second scripts although 20 and 40 second scripts are also used. If a script doesn't say a time, check with the client before recording!

TV ads are normally 30 seconds but due to the way TV operates, the ad will need to be spoken in 29 seconds.

It's good practice to be aware of how fast a 30 second script is and to learn this reading pace. Take a silent stopwatch with you for each session to refer to. It's very common to find a script over-written, which means you'll need to practise how you can compromise your diction to speed up your pace. You'll find you'll need to run two words into one such as "wan'to join us" instead of "want to join us" and "do not" to "don't". When you're talking more quickly you'll probably need to be more animated, so that the sentences still sound natural at a fast pace. Talking very quickly in an ordinary tone can sound like you're rushing. Use tone to add emphasis if you do not have the luxury of pausing or elongating words.

Chapter 9

Advice for Directed Sessions

9.1   What type of direction will I get from a producer?

Producers rely on voiceovers who can take direction well, so this is crucial for repeat bookings. Firstly, never argue with a producer as they have a clear idea of what they want, so go with the flow. The session will finish once they're happy so it's in everybody's best interest for you to follow their advice. A producer will generally be looking at the style of read, but also script timing. Most direction should be self-explanatory but you'll hear terms such as:

- Close mic – Less voice projection and being closer to the microphone gives a more personal and deeper sound.

- You're off mic – You are not aligned with the front of the mic or you are too far away from it and sound distant.

- You're popping – Sounds such as "B" and "P" (plosives) can create wind noise when spoken directly into the microphone.

- Contract the words – If there are words like "we will", the producer may prefer you to say "we'll" to make the read flow better.

- Lipsmacks and clicks – These are mouth noises and can be the result of a dry mouth. Some voices believe drinking tea and coffee before a session can cause these issues.

- Lift it up/brighter – If you smile while you read, you can lift the script and make it sound friendlier. Don't talk with a constant grin though, as you can have too much of a good thing and it will sound unnatural!

- Can you bring out... – The producer may ask you to put special emphasis on certain words.

- Can I have a pickup on... – A pickup is often a re-take of a small part of the script. This can be due to a slip up by you, or a script change.

- It's a 30 second read – Commercials have strict timings which are best checked prior to the session. During the session you may be asked to speed up or slow down. Having a silent stopwatch on-hand will help. Bear in mind a 30 second ad will probably require the read to come within 29 seconds.

- You dropped out or there was a glitch – ISDN can sometimes be unreliable and so you may need to do another take if the line momentarily fails and the producer loses audio.

9.2   Shall I record an ISDN session?

ISDN sessions are normally recorded at the "remote" studio by the producer, so there's no need to record an ISDN session. However on rare occasions you may be asked to record the session as a backup. Although it doesn't happen very often, it would be beneficial to ensure your studio setup will allow this.

If you're new to the industry, consider recording the sessions so you can listen back and critique yourself. It's also useful to keep these sessions for demo material, if you're unable to get a copy of the final mixdown.

9.3   What can I expect from my first ISDN session?

An ISDN session allows you to be directed and recorded by a producer in a remote studio. Commonly used within the commercial radio market, a producer will normally send a script and arrange a time when he/she will dial into your studio using ISDN.

Don't expect the producer to be always on time; it's not uncommon for sessions to start a few minutes late as the previous session may have overrun. Just keep your cool and help yourself by not packing your diary too tightly.

When you first start chatting to a producer on ISDN, you may hear yourself back in delay. This is because your voice is coming out of the producer's speakers and back into their microphone. This can be quite off-putting but when you record the actual script the producer will switch off their microphone, stopping the loop back.

It's good practice to read the script through prior to the session, so you can start by asking any questions relating to pronunciation or timing. Bear in mind that the producer will have a clear idea of how they want the recording to sound, so you'll often be required to voice through the script a few times. Sometimes the end client will also be listening in and may provide additional feedback. Some voices prefer being directed via ISDN rather than an offline recording, because the producer will approve the recording there and then once they're happy.

Before you start the main read you'll probably be asked to give some "level" which means the producer wants you to read a few lines as you would in the proper recording, to set their recording level. Don't be put off by requests for additional takes when you think you've delivered your best. Doing many takes is often not a reflection on your ability, but rather that the producer/director is covering all angles.

9.4   Should I make suggestions for the script?

Always read the script as it is written unless it's an obvious typo. On some occasions, producers will ask for your opinion. Be honest, but don't be overly critical; perhaps suggest doing it the way it's written, as well as another way, so the producer has all bases covered. A good way to play it if you're convinced there's a better way to say something is to wait until the producer is already happy with a take "as written". Once they have that in the bag, you can make a suggestion knowing that they already have a take they're pleased with.

9.5 How should I prepare for an in-person session?

For this type of session the client may expect to give you the script upon arrival. However it's a good idea to ask for it prior to the meeting to give you some time to prepare.

Always allow yourself plenty of time so you don't arrive late and be prepared by taking the contact name and number of the person you're meeting, in case you get delayed.

Use your appearance/dress sense to enhance your brand. For example don't dress too formally if you're a young and funky voice.

Try not to be intimidated upon arrival. You may be walked immediately into the booth to find yourself staring through a piece of glass at the engineer, director, agency staff and the end client! Remember they hired you because of your voice talents. They already like you or else they wouldn't have chosen you, so relax and perform as you would on any occasion, just as if you were in the booth on your own.

Try not to be put off or offended if they want you to read the lines over and over. We've been in sessions where the client hears what they want after just a few reads and we've also been in sessions where they want it spoken 10, 30 or even 50 times! You have to remember that some campaigns cost a small fortune so they want to make sure it's perfect. Don't get frustrated if it's a long session; if you feel you need a recess for five minutes to get a drink and fresh air, just ask at a convenient point.

If you've been booked directly, you should take additional business cards, but don't bring copies of your demo or try to turn it into a marketing opportunity.

If you've been booked via your agent, they should have provided you with all the details that you need. Any additional questions the client has regarding the booking, rates or repeat work should be directed back to your agent (or person who booked you).

The session may overrun, so ensure you have some contingency in your travel plans. It's standard practice to charge for overruns, but additional fees would only be charged for your studio time, and any usage fee would remain the same. Studio time is typically charged for an hour to begin with, then commonly by additional 30 minute slots. Agree your fee structure prior to the session as you don't want to talk money halfway through a recording.

From a safety perspective, it's wise to only operate out of recognised studio facilities. Be sensible and do your research if someone books you to appear at a specific address.

9.6   How do I ensure that I don't miss bookings during a session?

Producers appreciate that you may be unavailable to take calls if you are in a recording, so don't worry if you miss telephone calls during short sessions. Do ensure that you have an answer machine and your message provides alternative methods of contact, such as your mobile/email address. If you are recording on location, it's wise to forward your landline to your mobile. If you think you will be unavailable to take phone calls for more than a couple of hours, it's helpful to change your answer phone message with this information. Invest in a mobile device that also allows you to check your emails.

If you're going on holiday, warn regular clients in advance and ensure that you've set up an auto responder on your email account, as well as updating your answer phone.

9.7   Will eating and drinking before a session affect my voice?

The answer is yes. What you eat and drink, along with the temperature of the food/drink, will affect your vocal chords or make your tummy rumble. Everyone is different, so it may be a case of trial and error to find what affects you. It's common to find that hot drinks such as tea and coffee will have a negative impact. Other voices will swear that lemon drinks, honey or throat sweets will have a positive impact. There are no rules, just experiment yourself.

Do have a bottle of water with you in case you have a dry mouth in the middle of a session.

9.8   How do I deal with overwritten scripts?

The first thing to do if you think there is a problem is to raise the issue. Give the client or producer the opportunity to rewrite and come back to you with a better script. It's always good practice to check through scripts immediately after you receive them, even if you are not scheduled to record them yet.

If the script is overwritten but possibly feasible, follow some of these tips.

To "speed read" a script, don't just jump in and attempt it. Start by reading the script at a natural pace until you are comfortable with the message. You will familiarise yourself with the script and the approach you are going to take. Try to use pitch to emphasise words as you won't have the luxury of pausing or elongating them, then repeat the script, speeding up each time. If you are making an offline recording, you will probably want to record all these takes in case the client can time stretch, cut out breaths or change the duration required (by changing a 20 second ad into a 30 second ad or stretching visuals).

There are software techniques available which allow you to time stretch audio. It's not a magic solution though, as more than 10% or so of stretching will make the recording sound very unnatural. It would normally be the responsibility of the producer to time stretch recordings, although increasingly voice artists are offering this service as they become more tech savvy. Never time stretch recordings without telling your client or without providing the unstretched version as well.

9.9 Session tips

- Change the formatting of your script so that it's 1.5 or double line spaced; you may find it improves your sight reading.

- If printing doubled sided, make sure sentences don't run over the page.

- Don't be ashamed to have pride in your work. If you feel you haven't delivered your best or the director is pushing you into a bad read, be polite and just ask whether you can give another take but don't push it.

- Bad copy is normally only an issue if you don't read and mark up your script prior to the session.

- Don't turn your headphones up too loud, as they may be picked up by the microphone. If you find that you have to have your headphones very loud, you may want to consult a doctor to see whether you've excess ear wax!

- If you share the booth, ensure no other headphones are plugged in as they can cause feedback.

- Have a bottle of water at the ready so that you don't interrupt the session to get a drink.

- Be sensible with clothing. You don't want to be interrupting the session to take off layers because you're too hot.

- Take off watches, bangles and any jewellery that may make noise.

- Be prepared for last minute script changes. Have a spare piece of paper, pen and highlighter.

- Don't book your sessions back to back if you can help it. It then means you can cope with overruns and technical issues, as well as have a break between sessions.

- Avoid talking about session fees if the end client is present.

The producer/agency is likely to have marked up your cost so respect the supply chain.

- For an ISDN session, you may wish to begin by playing music down the line so the producer can hear when they connect to you.

- Learn to switch "voiceover mode" on and off. Occasionally you'll be under the weather or having a bad day, but when you step in the booth to talk to a producer remember your brand and your image. Stay professional at all times.

- Be friendly with regular producers but keep it businesslike. Don't burden them with your personal problems or get caught in the scenario where they feel obliged to ask how your cat is. Studio time is precious and schedules might be tight, so if they feel they need to chat for ten minutes before each recording with you, they may be reluctant to book you again.

Chapter 10

Improving Your Voice Quality

10.1   Can you recommend any tongue twisters?

Tongue twisters are fun and can also help train your mouth to move from one tricky sound to another. Try to perform these whilst sticking to your normal style and accent.

- A proper copper coffee pot.
- Around the rugged rocks the ragged rascals ran.
- Amidst the mists and coldest frosts,

  With stoutest wrists and loudest boasts,

  He thrusts his fist against the posts,

  And still insists he sees the ghosts.
- The sixth sick Sheik's sixth sheep is sick (supposed to be the hardest tongue twister in English language).
- Six sick slick slim sycamore saplings.
- A big black bug bit a big black bear, made the big black bear bleed blood.
- Vincent vowed vengeance very vehemently.
- Twelve twins twirled twelve twigs.
- Six shimmering sharks sharply striking shins.
- Can you imagine an imaginary menagerie manager imagining managing an imaginary menagerie?
- Pick a partner and practise passing, for if you pass proficiently, perhaps you'll play professionally.
- She stood upon the balustraded balcony, inexplicably mimicking his hiccupping.
- Lesser leather never weathered wetter weather better.
- Many an anemone sees an enemy anemone.
- He lifts the rocks to find his socks and hide them from the dusty clocks.
- Red lorry, yellow lorry.
- We'll weather the weather whatever the weather whether we like it or not.

10.2   How can I improve my enunciation?

Practising the common sounds of vowels and consonants is a good place to start.

Common vowel sounds:

- Ay as in day
- Ee as in see
- I as in pie
- Oh as in doh
- Oo as in you
- a as in cat
- e as in bed
- i as in nip
- o as in cog
- u as in but.

Once you've run through these vowel sounds you can add a consonant to the front of them and run through the list. Don't always use the same consonants as different letters require different mouth actions. For example a "W" would require you to loosen your lips whereas a "D" would require you to tighten your lips.

An example with "D":

Day, Dee, Di, Doh, Doo, Damp, Debt, Dig, Dot, Duck and so on with other consonants.

This can be useful as a warm up before a session to get your lips and tongue up to speed. It's also worth recording this exercise on regular occasions to listen back for general clarity; lisping and sibilance; whether it's breathy or forced and consistent in volume. You can go a step further by running through the table with an upwards, then a downwards inflection and so on.

You'll find a vocal coach will be able to help if you have specific areas to work at.

Mouth muscles are very small, so to exercise and strengthen them you'll need to over-exaggerate movements. You can find an item called a "bone prop" to help make movements on exercises bigger, but this isn't essential.

For more information try searching online for:
  enunciation exercises

10.3   Which words commonly cause problems?

There are many words that the general public will say incorrectly, but as a voiceover artist you need to be an expert in this area and not fall into the same traps.

Here are some common mistakes:

- Temperature – Don't miss the middle e.

- Temporary – Don't miss the o.

- Arctic/Antarctic – Remember to sound the first c.

- Espresso – Not expresso.

- February – Remember the first r.

- Forte – Correctly spoken as for-tay.

- Jewellery – Remember the w, don't say jool-ree.

- Library – Ly-bra-ree, not ly-bree.

- Sherbet – Not sherbert with a second r.

- Tenterhooks – Not tenderhooks.

- Utmost – Not upmost.

- Voluptuous – Not volumptuous with an m added.

- Government – Don't miss the first n.

This is by no means an exhaustive list but we wanted to make the point. Always read your scripts carefully as it's your responsibility to get these right.

10.4   Which Americanisms should I know about?

When reading a script for an American producer, client or audience, you should check whether they want words spoken in a more traditional English way, or in a style more palatable for an American market.

Some words to consider:

- Innovative – Inno-va-tive/inno-vay-tive
- Nougat – Noo-gar/noo-gat
- Aluminium – Aliminium/aluminum
- Research – Re-search/ree-search
- Resource – Re-source/ree-source
- Economic – Eck-o-nomic/eek-o-nomic
- Either – Eye-ther/ee-ther
- Neither – N'eye-ther/nee-ther
- Integral – In-tegg-ral/inter-gral
- Router – Roo-ter/row-ter
- Schedule – Skedule/shedule
- Patent – Pat-ent/pay-tent
- Default – De-fault/dee-fault
- Kilogram – Kill-o-gram/kee-lo-gram
- Micrometer – Micro-meter/my-crom-eter
- Insulation – Ins-yoo-lay-shun/in-sull-ay-shun

We've provided a simplified phonetic guide here. Just look in any dictionary if you want to refer to them in international phonetic alphabet form.

Some Americanisms have become acceptable in day to day conversation, so make note of how you normally say them. The most important issue is consistency across your recordings and certainly within the same script.

10.5 Why is posture and breathing important?

Having good posture is vital to allow proper controlled breathing. Your shoulders should be back and down with your chest up and out. Relax and you should feel your spine take on a natural curvature. Avoid slouching and tightening up.

By default we tend to take shallow "chest" breaths using only a small volume of our lungs. You'll find the time it takes you to breathe in is pretty much the same as the time it takes to breathe out. When voicing you're required to take a short efficient intake of breath and a slow controlled release of breath. This will allow you to voice for longer before running out of breath and to be able to breathe when it suits the script, rather than when you need to. You may hear that singers practise controlled breathing to increase their vocal range and this also applies to voiceover work.

10.6 How do I know whether I'm breathing properly?

Controlled breathing is sometimes called diaphragmatic breathing. Your diaphragm or "breathing muscle" is just inside the ribs and moves down to create more space for the lungs to expand.

You'll know whether you're breathing with your diaphragm because your belly will expand out as you breathe in. Then, similar to a bag pipe, you can control the air to release slowly as you speak. Test this by lying on the floor with one hand on your belly and one hand on your chest. As you inhale you should feel your belly rise. Continue to breathe in and your chest will also expand.

To compare, try reading a script using shallow breaths and then again with full breaths. Mark the point at which you breathe with different colour highlighter pens on your script. If you're doing it correctly, you should find you can last longer when using your diaphragm. Once comfortable with deeper breathing, it will become more economic, less intrusive and you'll be more relaxed. The sound will be formed using your whole chest and therefore affected by your body size and shape. Your voice will sound richer and fuller than if you use shallow breaths.

10.7   What should I expect from a vocal coach?

Before you book a session with a vocal coach do some research to ensure that they're the right type of coach for you.

- What qualifications do they have?
- Do they come recommended?
- Are they a speech therapist or a vocal coach?
- Do they specialise in singing or speaking?

Vocal coaches should all be able to advise on a few general areas such as confidence building, breathing techniques, eliminating bad habits and the basic care and maintenance of your voice, so that you can sustain a comfortable speaking voice over a long period.

More importantly they should help you "find your voice". That may sound a bit of a cliché, but a good vocal coach will help you explore various styles and focus their attention on those which suit you best.

Don't forget that you're paying them, so if you have something you want to improve on, just mention it. If you were asked to record a script in a natural style and the client thought you sounded too much like a voiceover, then ask to work on that. Or perhaps they might suggest any remedies for physical issues, such as getting a very dry mouth during a session.

Some vocal coaches will offer a more traditional approach, advising on "correct" vowel and consonant pronunciation, which may aim to reduce a regional accent. Be careful not to lose your individuality as you could lose your unique selling point.

10.8   What is a "nasal voice" and how can I avoid it?

A nasal voice occurs when your voice reverberates throughout your nose cavities more than your mouth. It is generally considered not very appealing and so if you find your voice is a little nasal you may wish to work on this area.

At the back of your mouth there's a spongy muscle called the soft palate. You can feel it move when you say the sounds "ahhhh" (should not be nasal at all) and "nnnngggg" (should reverberate more in your nose). To avoid a nasal voice, practise relaxing your mouth when speaking, so you're closer to the "ahhhh" position than the "nnnnggg" position. If you can't solve the problem yourself it's best to consult a vocal coach. See the previous question for more information.

10.9   How do I reduce noisy breathing?

Noisy breathing is made worse by bad posture and by not relaxing your belly as you speak. If your belly is rigid, the air will sound like it is being scraped in. So relax and work on your posture. Please see Question 10.6 "How do I know whether I'm breathing properly?" and the relaxation exercise at the end of this chapter.

If, despite all this, you still find intrusive breaths on your recordings, you could try what one of our engineers calls the "swimming technique". This is the action of turning your head slightly to the side when you breathe, as if you were doing front crawl, so that you're not directly facing the microphone when you inhale.

Producers may favour voices who don't require a lot of de-breathing as it cuts down on their work load.

10.10 I have a speech impediment. Does this mean I can't be a voiceover artist?

It's fair to say that a speech impediment can restrict your marketability, as it could detract from the message being put across. However some voices find that their speech impediment is marketable or endearing and find it actually becomes their unique selling point – think of Jonathan Ross.

There is no clear right or wrong, but it's important not to disguise it on your demo audio otherwise the producer will get a surprise after recording you and may not be too happy.

Many speech impediments can be reduced. Lisping is caused when the tongue is too close to the teeth. A weak "R" means the tongue is not being used effectively. Consult a speech therapist for specific advice on your particular situation.

10.11 How can I take care of my voice?

This is mainly common sense. Smoking, dehydration and shouting can all damage your voice. If you have a healthy lifestyle, eating nutritionally, exercising and most importantly relaxing and sleeping well, then your voice should be at its best.

If you find your voice is drying up, consider the use of a steamer as this will provide subtle moisture to your vocal cords.

Consider a daily stretching routine, learning yoga or other relaxation techniques, and learn how to breathe properly.

Some voices avoid or restrict their intake of caffeine so consider reducing your consumption of tea and coffee. Others drink warm water with honey and lemon as a replacement.

Remember your vocal cords are like a rubber band, so drinking very cold or very hot liquids may negatively affect them.

> TIP:
> If a script contains a "shouty" section or something that you think may strain your voice temporarily, it's advisable to record this section at the end of the session.

10.12 What is the Alexander Technique and its relevance?

Frederick Alexander was an Australian actor who suffered from chronic laryngitis when he performed. He devised his own solution when his doctors could not help. He became aware that tension in his neck and body were causing his problems and refined a technique to help others.

The Alexander Technique aims to improve awareness of bad and good posture. Good posture, not slouching or being too rigid, will help you speak and breathe most effectively.

Although there are books and videos on the subject, the best way of learning the Alexander Technique is to be taught in person. If you are interested, find a local course or tutor.

10.13 I have a sharp "SS" sound when I speak. What can I do?

Don't worry if it's not too extreme. Sibilance is a fairly familiar problem, and there are things you can do.

Sibilance can be caused by tongue placement and gaps in your teeth, which you may be able to improve.

You can also treat the problem technically by purchasing a "De-esser" box which can soften strong "SS" sounds on the fly. Be careful not to filter out your "SS" sound too much though, as a clear "SS" is important for clarity.

You can also filter and soften strong "SS" sounds after recording, using a good audio software package. It's easily configurable and the benefit of this method is that you can undo any changes and retry if you think the setting is too weak or too strong.

10.14 Can you recommend a relaxation exercise?

NOTE: Always consult a doctor before starting any new exercise program.

1) Lay down on the floor facing upwards and close your eyes.

2) Relax your shoulders and feel them loosen and drop.

3) Breathe in deeply right down to your belly. Slowly exhale.

4) Repeat five times.

5) Open your eyes and stand up in your own time.

6) Relax your neck and tilt your head back slowly.

7) Bring your head back to centre slowly, then gently tilt forward.

8) Again, return to centre slowly.

9) Do the same, gently tilting to the right, then back to centre and again to the left, then back to centre.

Chapter 11

Voiceover Rates

11.1   Where can I find a list of voiceover rates?

As a voice artist, you are probably freelance and so have the freedom to set your own rates. With any business you must begin with some market research to find out what your competitors are charging so you can pitch yourself at the going rate. There is advice at the ready for members of Equity if you're struggling to set your fees. They're on hand via phone or email for specific job quotes in a broad spectrum of the market. Check out Question 1.9 "Do I need to join Equity?".

Many experienced voice artists are concerned about new artists coming into the market and pitching their fees too low, either to get the work or because they're not sure what to charge. Many feel this may cause a downward spiral in prices, which would eventually mean that rates would be too low for voice artists to sustain themselves in the quiet periods. If in doubt, it's best to err on the side of caution and set your rates higher, then be prepared to be knocked down.

11.2   What is a buyout?

Clients will use the term "buyout" but this sometimes means different things to different people. For example do they actually mean they want a licence to use the recording on any radio station within a certain period of time, or do they want a licence to use it on a single radio station but for an unlimited time? We don't advise voiceover artists to completely sign over the rights to their recordings, so that they may be used on any platform, for an unlimited amount of time. So if you're asked for a buyout, try to restrict the use in some way.

If a client asks for a buyout, we think it's fair for the voiceover to ask what their budget is. You should then offer usage terms that you would feel comfortable with for this budget. For example unlimited use on UK satellite TV but for six months only.

Ask for a copy of the script, as this may indicate a natural shelf life for the recording. Let's say they're advertising a winter sale for a specific range of beds. It's unlikely that the same range of beds would be available in their next winter sale.

11.3   Is undercutting bad?

Being a self-employed voiceover, care should be taken not to undervalue the work that you do.

It's important to find out the going rate for each particular job and be competitive to a degree. The danger comes if you're unaware of the going rate and pitch yourself way below your competitors. You're actually devaluing your own services and it will be harder for you to achieve the going rate for future projects. It's better for casting decisions to be made on voice choice rather than budget; this way whoever gets the job will be paid the market value. If a new client is limited by budget and you wish to still do the work, make it clear that it's an introductory offer so as not to devalue your services. Be careful, however, that you're not being taken advantage of and the company isn't trying this with everyone.

Clients and creative producers value choice in the industry. If rates are kept low, budgets become inflexible over time. Niche or specialist voices who are only hired for an occasional job would not be able to support themselves on the lower rate and may leave the industry. This results in less choice and creativity can suffer. A perfect example of this can be found within the local radio market in the UK. For example if a station pays £25 for a 30 second commercial and requires a genuine Italian voice for a new restaurant, they'll find it difficult to hire an Italian voice.

Remember there's a supply chain, so you may wish to offer more competitive rates or a fixed discount for companies who are reselling you to their clients and need room to make a profit themselves.

11.4 How do I cost up local radio and in-store ads?

In local radio, producers tend to follow the Equity guidelines which provide "minimum" rates for local radio commercials. The rates are banded for each radio station and accumulate if the script/recording is for broadcast on more than one station. These rates are just a guideline for members of Equity, although it is fairly uncommon for voiceovers to charge more than these minimum rates. There are actually two Equity radio rate cards: one if you're being booked by an ad agency, and another for everything else. The ad agency rates specify a minimum session fee and the per station rate is generally higher.

Some voices will charge an additional fee if the commercial is recorded by themselves and sent as an MP3 file (as opposed to an ISDN session). An extra fee is normally applicable if the end client listens in to the recording session.

Here's an example dialogue for a local radio booking:

Client: Hi Ben, got a 30 second ad for you. It's going on Radio Plymouth and Exeter FM. Are you Equity rate?

Voiceover: Thanks, yeah I'm Equity rate. What time do you want me? I'm free in 20 minutes at 10.15am if that's cool?

Client: Great, speak to you then!

Voiceover: Lovely, please can you send over your address and I'll email you the invoice after the session if that's okay?

Comments: If you don't work to common local radio rates and the producer doesn't ask, they may be assuming that you do, so always clarify your rates before recording.

This example is for illustrative purposes only. We cannot provide specific rate guidance so please set your own rates.

11.5   How do I cost up corporate jobs?

The term "corporate" is often used for many miscellaneous voice jobs such as web videos, e-learning, presentation narrations, software and hardware systems, and anything else aimed more towards the business to business market.

If your client has booked a studio for you to record in, then you will probably charge an hourly rate – your basic session fee (BSF). If you are recording using your own studio, it's common to quote based on the script length. One method is to estimate the time taken to record and set your fee based on your hourly BSF. For example if you estimate the script will take 30 minutes you may charge half your BSF. It's common practice to have a minimum rate; some voices will not charge less than their full BSF for corporate work.

If the recording is going to get high exposure, then you should be able to negotiate a usage fee. A usage fee is basically a licence for the client to use your recording for a specific high profile use.

Here are some example dialogues for corporate bookings:

Example 1:
Client: Hello, I heard your demo on your website and wanted a quote for the health and safety script attached. We'd just need it as an MP3 sometime this week. Do you include changes? The client may alter a few sentences when they hear it back.

Voiceover: Great to hear from you, the script is around 10 minutes finished narration and I'd cost this at my normal corporate rate of £250+VAT. I'd charge £50+VAT for subsequent updates (up to 10% of the original word count) if recorded in a single pickup session. I've attached a sample of something similar I recorded recently – is that style OK for you?

Client: That's perfect, I'll let you know when the team chooses a voice.

Example 2:
Client: Hello Mark, we're an events company putting together an award ceremony for one of our clients. They've asked us how much it would be to use a professional voice for the intro to the awards ceremony after the meal. There's a short script, around 100 words, to say welcome. Could you let me know how much this would be for an MP3 on email?

Voiceover: Thanks for your enquiry, great to hear from you. Please can you let me know whether the audio will only be used on this night? Also can you confirm it won't be televised or used on the web later?

Client: Yeah it's just single use on that night. If we got the script tomorrow, how quickly would you be able to record?

Voiceover: I could do that tomorrow afternoon to return by close of play. I can record a couple of takes and this would be within my minimum fee of £150.

Example 3:
Client: Hello, Julie, it's me again. We have a new product coming out that's a talking Christmas tree. We have 25 phrases to record.

Voiceover: Hi, thanks for your message. Do you just want a WAV file as normal? Also how many units are going to be sold or made?

Client: Actually the client would like to listen in so probably ISDN, no more than an hour. They're expecting to make approx 15,000 units.

Voiceover: Excellent, the world will be a better place with 15,000 talking trees! I'd cost this at £225 for an hour ISDN session plus 100% for the usage up to 15,000 units. Then if they decide to do another run can you let me know and we'll charge an additional 100%.

Client: Sounds great. I'll email you in a couple of days to confirm.

Example 4:

Client: Hello, we're a London ad agency and we're producing a web video for one of our clients. The video is around three minutes but I don't have a script yet. What are your rates for web videos?

Voiceover: Hi, thanks for thinking of me. If you don't need to listen in to the recording I can cost this up as follows...

Up to five minutes for small/medium business to business online: £250.

Up to five minutes for large company business to business: £350.

Up to five minutes for large company, public facing: £250 plus 100% usage online for up to 12 months.

Client: Perfect, I'll let you know if they choose your voice.

These examples are for illustrative purposes only. We cannot provide specific rate guidance so please set your own rates.

11.6   How do I cost up telephone on-hold prompts?

A telephone on-hold prompt is a short paragraph (a couple of sentences, normally no more than 50 words) which will be used on a company's telephone system and looped when the caller is on hold. It's common for a company to have a number of messages/prompts. If you're quoting to a company who make telephone on-hold productions, you would normally charge a "per prompt" rate, with a minimum number of prompts; for example £5 per prompt, with a minimum of ten prompts. If you are working directly with the company using your recording, you will also need to take into account possible extra costs due to editing etc.

Here is an example dialogue for an on-hold booking:

Client: Hello, Ben, I've got five telephone prompts for you. What's your rate?

Voiceover: Great, have you got the script you can send over? Is it telephone on-hold or for an IVR menu?

Client: Just on-hold. It's for a small plumbing company in Pen-y-Bont.

Voiceover: Ooooh exciting, haha! I'm £5 per prompt but have a minimum booking of ten prompts so it'll be £50. Normally I class a prompt as up to 50 words but as there are only five it doesn't matter if they're a little over.

Client: Great, the script is attached so please go ahead and email back as MP3 mono 128k. Can you make sure it's 48kHz too please?

Voiceover: No problem. You'll have it by 3pm.

This example is for illustrative purposes only. We cannot provide specific rate guidance so please set your own rates.

11.7   How do I cost up telephone menu systems?

These recordings should not be confused with telephone on-hold prompts. The fee should be based on how much exposure you think the telephone menu is going to get. As an example, you may charge 50% of your BSF for a small script used by a small company, whereas you may charge no less than your BSF for a national or multinational company. Bear in mind that it may mean regular work through updates, so don't price yourself out. Be aware that some companies ask for specific exclusivity to prevent your voice being used on a competitor's phone system. This will limit work and thus you may be able to negotiate a higher rate.

Here is an example dialogue for an IVR booking:

Client: Hello, Ben, I've got 15 telephone prompts for you. What's your rate?

Voiceover: Great, have you got the script you can send over? Is it telephone on-hold or for an IVR menu?

Client: There's one on-hold message and 14 IVR menu prompts. I haven't got the script yet.

Voiceover: Okay, well can I assume it's for a small/medium business? In this case my rates are £5 for an on-hold message up to 50 words and £15 per menu prompt. If you can send over the script I'll confirm this.

Client: Yes, it's just for the paperweight centre in Leg O' Mutton, Devon. Would you be able to do it as a session for £200 total? I've attached the script and some of the prompts are very small.

Voiceover: Yeah, no problem. You've sent a few nice scripts my way this month, so happy to do a deal.

This example is for illustrative purposes only. We cannot provide specific rate guidance so please set your own rates.

Always find out whether the system is for a small/medium business or a national public facing service, which would have higher exposure, as you would charge an additional usage fee. Be careful not to agree on a session fee blindly on an estimate of "a few pages of prompts".

In our example the rates were lower than Ben would quote if dealing directly with the end client. This is because there's a supply chain and Ben's producer also needs a margin to mark up the sale of the recording. He's also likely to have more return work for Ben.

11.8   How do I cost up a documentary narration?

In most cases, documentary narrations are recorded in person and for an hour programme you can expect to be booked for a two to three hour session. Most voices will base their fees on their BSF; for example an hour documentary may be priced at two or three times your BSF. Do try to see whether you can negotiate more (such as an additional 100%) if it sounds like it's a high profile documentary e.g. BBC 1 or 2, ITV1, Channel 4.

Here is an example dialogue for a documentary narration booking:

Client: Hey, Jerry, we've got another docu script for you. It's a one hour programme as before. We've booked the usual Soho studio on Friday, 2–4pm – are you available?

Voiceover: Thanks, Sarah, I'm around all Friday at the moment if you want to confirm. Is it for satellite?

Client: Yeah, it's another in the "Killer worms gone mad" series for N-light channel. Can I assume £500 as before?

Voiceover: Perfect, I'll hold the slot until close of play today. If you can let me know for definite by 5pm please?

This example is for illustrative purposes only. We cannot provide specific rate guidance so please set your own rates.

11.9 How do I cost up TV and national radio commercials?

For national TV, it's advised to obtain the TVRs (television ratings) and then plug your BSF into a usage calculator (such as can be found at www.usefee.tv). If TVRs are unavailable, ask for information on how long the campaign is to run for and which channels. Also try to gauge whether it's going to be high profile by checking the script for brand names. Do your research with this as some TV recordings can be worth £10,000 upwards. For short-run TV commercials broadcast in a single region, some voices charge their BSF plus 100% for usage. For national radio, most producers will expect to pay rates based on Equity guidelines. If you also follow Equity guidelines, check whether it's an ad agency booking and refer to the correct rate card.

Here are some example dialogues for TV commercial bookings:

Example 1:
Client: Hi, Jane, we're looking to put you forward for a TVC. Can you let me know your availability and BSF please for a single 30 second script?

Voiceover: Hey, thanks, please put me forward. I'm not going anywhere over the next couple of weeks. Is this an in-person session in central London? My usual BSF is £225 for these sessions and I normally base the usage on the TVRs. Is this good for you?

Client: Sure, the TVRs won't be any more than 100 which calculates to £1,892.25.

Voiceover: Great, let me know how it goes! Thanks again and I'm happy to do a custom sample if it helps the client decide.

Example 2:

Client: Hi, Jane, we're looking to put you forward for a TVC. We need a buyout and it's a single 30 second. Budget is limited, I'm afraid; we've got £600. Can you let me know if you want me to suggest you?

[Voiceover checks client's website to see whether it's a big ad agency and what clients they normally work with. She finds out that it's a regional ad agency with some local clients.]

Voiceover: Do you need me in person? If there's a budget I can do a better price on ISDN. What channels do you need a buyout for and how long is the campaign? Is it on all UK regions?

Client: ISDN should be fine for this one. It's going to be on two satellite kids channels for three months (KidzAction and KidzCartoon).

Voiceover: Okay sounds fair for the exposure. Happy to be put forward at £600 if recorded on ISDN – let me know if you want a custom demo for the client as I'm around all day.

These examples are for illustrative purposes only. We cannot provide specific rate guidance so please set your own rates.

11.10 Should I offer a discount for bulk recordings?

Yes, in many businesses it's perfectly acceptable to offer a client a fair discount for large orders. However some clients will often request a discounted rate on an expectation or promise of plenty of work. Unfortunately, too often you'll find the work won't materialise and any discount was not really fair. Perhaps they have a new business idea and their expectations of work level are "optimistic".

There are a couple of approaches to consider which are "win/win" if the client has accurately predicated the work load.

1) Use a sliding scale. For example a client comes to you with a script that you'd normally charge £150 for and requests that you record it for £75 as he "expects" there to be about 40 of them. It would be better to say that you'll do the first 10 for £150 per script, the next 10 for £75, and the final 20 for £37.50 per script. This way, the client gets the value they wanted for the large booking, but you're protected from the start if the work doesn't materialise.

2) Use a retainer. For example a client expects ten scripts a month, which would normally cost £100 in isolation, but he would like to pay £50 per script considering the regular work. Instead of recording the scripts at £50 each, offer a monthly fee structure of £500 per month, for up to ten scripts.

With both situations you'd probably want to cap the word count or session time if you're being directed. Give the client some room for the natural ebb and flow of script sizes and negotiate what you both think is fair.

Chapter 12

The Future of Voiceovers

12.1 How is the voiceover market likely to develop?

Experience has shown the following trends, which look likely to continue:

- Wider selection of accents and styles of voice are available for producers. Long gone are the days when all voiceover artists were neutral accented announcers.

- More applications/platforms which utilise voice recordings.

- More broadcast channels/stations/networks.

- Tighter budgets due to advertising revenues dropping.

- Technology becoming cheaper in the industry and barriers to entry lowering.

- More potential of work, but rates being watered down.

- More emphasis on speed of delivery and cost.

- Improved opportunities from the global marketplace.

- The physical location of a voice artist becoming increasingly irrelevant.

- Less requirement or budget for in-person recordings.

- Voiceover artists becoming increasingly computer and technologically literate.

- Increased remote auditioning for work via MP3.

- Voiceovers increasingly being recorded from home studios.

We think the industry is going to be exciting and rewarding for those voiceover artists who are able to move with the times, and keep marketing and improving their talents.

12.2   Will "text to speech" systems make the market redundant?

Text to speech (TTS) is a method where a real voice will record a set of sentences, which are then analysed and processed by a computer algorithm. The resulting processing means the computer can take a set of sentences and create speech fairly accurately using the pre-recorded elements.

Computers are far from being able to add feeling and true meaning to scripts, so we don't believe that we'll ever see the days when computers are used to voice adverts, commercials or even corporate scripts.

However the system is useful in situations where it would not normally be feasible to use a voice artist, such as reading emails aloud for blind people.

12.3   How can I prepare myself for the future?

Consider these tips:

- Ensure you are well connected when someone tries to get hold of you and that you can access your emails and diary wherever you are. You may not be available all the time, but you can be responsive and book in jobs.

- Set up your home studio, or if you already have a home studio, periodically request feedback and improve the sound quality.

- Teach yourself simple editing and sound processing.

- Establish/advertise yourself globally.

- Use all the latest online social networking sites for marketing and PR.

- Invest in a mobile studio setup so you can be available when you're on holiday. This way you have the option to do the odd demo or important pickup for valued clients.

Chapter 13

Tips to Make You Stand Out

13.1 What tips can you give to make me better than the competition?

1.   For undirected sessions build a reputation for error free recordings. Always proof your recordings before delivering.

2.   Availability is crucial, so when you're not available, make sure you set your answer machine and email auto reply. This way, producers are never in doubt as to when you're next available for work.

3.   Improve your studio sound. Producers really appreciate good quality audio and better sound could give you the edge over a similar voice.

4.   Show your appreciation to a producer who gives you work. Some voices act like they're doing the producer a favour, but offer your thanks and remember they are the customer.

5.   Be organised with your invoices/payments. Hassling producers for a purchase order two months after a session makes work difficult for them. Make it easy for them to pay you.

6.   Be open to providing free samples and auditions for work. Some clients can't hear that you're flexible from a generic demo, so show them you can do the job. You can also prove your studio quality and turnaround time by being responsive with samples, even when they're not asked for.

7.   Get a reputation for being easy-going, approachable and fair with rates. You may have a minimum session fee, but being non-negotiable will put producers off considering you for jobs that may only be a fraction lower than your usual rate.

8.   As well as being bookable direct, try to get other people to resell your services. This may be through a traditional agency or via a website such as www.voiceovers.co.uk. The more shop fronts you have, the more bookings you're likely to receive.

9.   Improve your knowledge of computers and audio formats. If you know your AIFFs from your WAVs and can deliver at 44.1kHz or 48kHz then you're on the same wavelength (sorry) as the people booking you.

10.   Make it easy for people who want to direct the session live. You can be London based or within travelling distance, you can have ISDN facilities, telephone patch, Source-Connect, Skype etc.

Appendix A

Sample Terms and Conditions

Terms and Conditions of Service (Dec 2010)

Booking title:

Date:

With reference to the recording named:

Voice artist "Me" or "I":

Company/licence holder "You":

Engagement

You engage me to commence with the booking/recording specified here with the terms defined here. The fee has been based on the script provided – if a different script is provided since this booking agreement I reserve the right to provide a revised fee/agreement.

Content

You warrant that the audio recording will only be used within the scope of the defined licence for use as agreed in my quote.

Assignment

After two months from audio delivery, you assign permission for me to use the recording in my own marketing. I do not assign complete rights for the recording to You – the recording is provided as per the defined licence for use. If additional usage is required, this should be covered by a separate booking agreement.

If usage terms are breached, I reserve the right to invoice for any additional usage backdated to the date of the usage breach and charge an administration fee of £75+VAT.

Payment

You agree to pay the agreed fee (plus VAT if applicable) on presentation of a valid invoice from me, which will be payable in accordance with terms specified in the booking agreement (normally 30 days).

Editing

The recording may be edited, modified, added to or deleted from, but the resultant audio will be licensed within the same scope as defined here.

Warranties

You warrant that nothing in the booking or script is obscene, libelous, blasphemous or infringes any performer's right, and performer's property right, any moral right, any right of copyright, right of privacy, right of publicity or any other right whatsoever of any third party.

Indemnity

You agree to indemnify me, my affiliates, officers, directors and employees against, and to keep me, my affiliates, officers, directors and employees indemnified from and against, all actions, proceedings, costs, claims, damages and demands however arising in respect of any actual or alleged breach or non-performance by You or any or all of the undertakings, warranties or obligations under this Agreement.

Pronunciations and recording style

You will endeavour to provide me with the correct pronunciations and required recording style more than one hour prior to the planned session commencement.

Re-record policy / problems

It's your responsibility to check the recording and notify me of any problems within five working days.

You have directed the session, or if a custom sample was

approved prior to the recording, then re-records after the session is complete will incur an additional expense and be covered under a separate booking agreement. The only exception would be if the audio delivery is corrupt, in which case I would endeavour to resolve the issue.

For an undirected session where a custom sample was not approved, I may agree to a single re-record session at my discretion if:

– The script and direction is unchanged.
– Pronunciations are consistent with that indicated by you prior to booking.
– I am notified within five days of the initial recording.
– The script is less than 1,000 words.

For scripts of more than 1,000 words, we recommend you request a custom sample and approve the style prior to me making the full recording.

Booking cancellation

Once a booking has been agreed, the fee may become payable in full whether or not the recording is still required. This fee would be representative of my costs because the studios may have been booked already, or I may have rejected other work. If I am ill or have a technical problem I may need to cancel or delay a booking. If I cancel a booking, the agreement will become void and a new agreement needs to be re-signed to cover the amended session.

Governing law

The governing law of this Agreement is English law and the parties submit to non-exclusive jurisdiction of the courts of England and Wales.

Appendix B

Sample Licence Agreement

Audio Licence Agreement (Dec 2010)

Recording title or reference:

Date:

Voice artist "Me" or "I":

Company/licence holder "You":

About this licence

The recording specified above has been made by recording my voice.

I do not assign complete rights of the recording to You – the recording is provided as per the following licence for use. If additional usage is required, a new or updated licence should be requested and the associated fee negotiated.

If the usage terms are breached, I reserve the right to invoice for any additional usage, backdated to the date of the usage breach, and charge an administration fee of £75+VAT.

Licence is given for the following uses (please specify):

Examples:
Internal corporate use, intranet, staff etc.
Business to business use, marketing, website
Public facing use

For the following duration (please specify if unlimited):

12 months, commencing from DATE

If commercial TV/radio broadcast, the following limitations apply:

Specify TVRs or list of stations/durations etc.

The recording may be included in a re-saleable product or service (yes or no)?

No

If yes, the product/service run is limited to the following units:

N/A

The recording itself is for the defined use outlined in this agreement and cannot be resold or given away to a third party.

The recording is strictly NOT licensed for the following uses (delete where appropriate):

Examples:
Public television or radio broadcast
Online website use
Telephone system use

Governing law

The governing law of this Agreement is English law and the parties submit to non-exclusive jurisdiction of the courts of England and Wales.

Appendix C

Sample Scripts

Sample commercial script – 30 seconds

Car screeches, bumps, sound of glass breaking

Ann. (natural, trusting and honest sounding):

Bump in the road? Locked your keys in the car? Or even just a chip from a stone?

Take the stress out of your car worries with Pane in the Glass.

Pane in the Glass offer free estimates on all your glass needs.

Unlike other companies, we won't leave you stranded. With roadside assistance 24/7 and more attendants during the work run, we're on hand when you need us most!

Call Pane in the Glass for your free quote. We'll be with you the same day or we'll fix your pane for free. Call 08080 700 007 now.

Sample telephone script

Ann. (clear, steady pace, friendly and natural):

Prompt 1

Hello, thanks for calling Roamer. Your calls may be recorded for quality and training purposes. Please listen carefully to the following options.

Prompt 2

Welcome to Roamer.
If you are on a monthly contract including Roam Free, press 1
If you are a Roaming Around broadband customer, press 2
If you are a Free Roaming customer, press 3
If you are a business customer, press 4
If you want more information about the recent changes to our rates, please press 5

Prompt 3

To hear your account balance or use a voucher, press 1
If you are having technical difficulties, press 2
If you are calling about something else, please press 3

Prompt 4

This line is dedicated to Roamer's recent rate changes.
If you would like more information about Roam Free rate changes, press 1
If you would like more information about Roaming Around rate changes, press 2
If you would like more information about Free Roaming rate changes, press 3
If you are a business customer, please press 4

Sample documentary script

Ann. (Serious, unemotional, unopinionated. Factual sounding):

It was mid 1941 and despite controlling the Western Front, Hitler turned back to the east to achieve what he saw as his prime objective – to invade and occupy Russia, which had prepared its huge military to launch a preemptive strike against him.

The Germans managed to catch Russia by surprise, but that was not enough to secure their victory.

Following Stalin's orders, the Russian intelligence made a huge effort to constantly monitor for any preparation by the German military to ready itself for the severe weather conditions of the Russian winter. Stalin saw this as being the clearest warning sign of an imminent German attack. However the Germans did not prepare, such was their confidence that the war against Russia would be won before winter, and so Stalin dismissed all warnings from Intelligence that Germany was about to attack. He did not believe Hitler would take such a wild gamble.

With surprise on their side, the invading German military caught the Russian army in a bad position. The Russian losses in men and equipment were tremendous. They also lost the entire vast territory between Poland and Moscow and the entire military force occupying at the time.

The advancing German army, aided by efficient tactical air support of the Luftwaffe which dominated the skies, advanced all the way to Moscow, but it was at that time, in the extreme winter of late 1941, that the German military ran out of time and energy.

The German soldiers were exhausted; pushed to their limits and already suffering badly from the winter. Russian reinforcements brought in from the other side of Russia, Siberia and the Far East chose this moment to counter-attack. The Russian military was perfectly equipped for extreme weather conditions and the advancing Germans were stopped, marking the limit of what the German military could achieve in the Eastern Front. They had great victories in Russia, but Russia, with its endless resources, large land mass, tough winter and tough soldiers, was too much for the Germans.

When the winter passed, the Germans advanced again, far and deep but not in the direction of Moscow. Despite their best efforts they had failed to defeat Russia.

Sample corporate script for website

(Formal style, but not stuffy – it's serious content but aimed at mums and dads):

With Vault internet security, it's so simple to protect your PC and your kids at the same time.

Our new parental controls feature allows you to easily customise kids' access so that you know what they can see, and when they can see it.

Just click and drag each user across the timetable to set your weekly usage plan.

Once done, click "confirm".

Now you have complete control over surfing times.

Next you'll be asked which accounts you'd like to "Vault".

Click to highlight each profile that you'd like to add protection to.

Select confirm and you'll be asked to set the filter level for each child.

Vault internet security's sophisticated statistical analysis allows the most comprehensive breakdown of usage.

If you want to review your stats you can instantly pull up the figures by clicking on "usage reports" in the main menu.

Alternatively, for weekly reports on usage, just tick "weekly reports" in the timetable menu.

Appendix D

Sample Invoice

Invoice

Mr V. Over
1 High Street
Cheddington
Bedfordshire
MK1 1AA

Voiceovers Ltd   01-01-2011
PO Box 326
Plymouth
Devon
PL4 9YQ

Invoice: VO-001   VAT number: GB012345678

PO	Price	VAT (17.5%)	Total
123/4	£150	£26.25	£176.25

Recording of health and safety module 1 for Rutland Council
17-12-2010. Booked by G. Smith.

Total	£150	£26.25	£176.25

[Single line description of usage and length of usage if not
agreed on a separate booking form.]

Payment terms: 30 days from receipt of invoice
BACS payments to be made to:
Mr. V. Over
Account 01234567
Sort code 01-23-45

PayPal address: mrvover@email.com

Tel: 01234 567890   victor_over@email.com

Glossary

Glossary

A

- Adobe Audition – A popular audio software package for recording/editing. Formally called "Cool Edit Pro".

- ADR – Automatic Dialogue Replacement. This is the process of replacing the voice track of a video with a new voice recording.

- Agent – Someone who acts on your behalf to pitch you for all or certain areas of your work. They deal with the contract/negotiation side of the process and take a percentage fee for their work. Some voices have multiple agents.

- AIFF or .aif – Stands for Audio Interchange File Format. It's commonly used on Macs rather than PCs as an alternative to a wave file as it's pretty much the same size and quality.

- A-law – A type of audio file optimised for use on embedded systems such as an IVR menu.

- Alt. or alt. take – An alternative read of a line or script.

- Alexander Technique – A technique that aims to improve your posture. See Question 10.12 "What is the Alexander Technique and its relevance?".

- Amplitude – The volume of a recording. To amplify is to increase the volume.

- Audacity – A popular free audio software package for recording/editing.

- Audio – A generic term relating to any sound or sound file.

- Auto responder – An email function which will send an automatic email on your behalf when you're away from your computer, to let clients know when you're back in the studio.

B

- Bed – The soundtrack or music laid under a voice recording.

- Bi-directional microphone – A microphone which is designed to pick up sound from both the front and the back of the microphone. It's used for double headers and interviews but is not really ideal for a single-voice recording.

- Bitrate – How many "bits" are processed per second (kilo bits per second) and in an audio file. Having a low bitrate will result in poor quality. For MP3 recordings you should deliver at 128 Kbps mono or higher. Don't think that 128 Kbps stereo is the same; it's actually equivalent to just 64 Kbps mono.

- Bleed through – When unwelcome sound breaks through onto a recording. This can occur if your headphones are too loud.

- Bone prop – A small bone shaped piece of plastic that you bite down on when doing mouth exercises to force exaggerated movements.

- Broadcast – Anything that's transmitted to the public but more commonly used for television and radio transmissions rather than online webcasts.

- BSF – Basic session fee (some people call this the basic studio fee) is the cost for an hour of your time in the studio. It does not include extra costs such as studio hire fees, editing and usage. It is used as the basis for working out quotes for TV and corporate jobs.

- Buyout – Describes the fee paid to a voiceover so a client can use a recording in an unrestricted way. The buyout could be for an unrestricted length of time but on just one platform/channel or it might be to use the recording on an unrestricted number of TV channels within a certain period of time. Sometimes it can mean to use anywhere for any length of time but this is not advised. Always check what a client means when they say "buyout".

C

- Cans – Another name for headphones.

- Cardioid microphone – The most common type of speech microphone for voice artists. It's named cardioid because the area/pattern where it picks up sound is heart shaped when pictured from above. They're good at rejecting sound from the rear of the microphone, hence the preference for recordings with a single voice.

- CD-R – A type of CD which allows you to make a permanent digital recording to the disc. It's advisable to have a generic set of CD-Rs printed with your main contact information.

- Channels – A mono recording would use a single channel where as a stereo recording would use two channels. A voiceover recording will generally be a single channel.

- Cheesy – An over the top, smiley, happy style. Like an overly happy radio presenter with a permanent grin.

- Colouration – A form of audio distortion.

- Compression (data) – In terms of audio storage, compression is the process of reducing the size of a file. For example an MP3 would be a compressed version of a wave file. Clever technology is used to try to prevent loss of quality noticeable to the human ear, but over-compressing will inevitably result in an audible degradation of sound.

- Compression (sound waves) – In terms of sound compression, this process will boost the lower parts of the sound wave and limit the louder parts. It brings the two volume extremes more tightly together.

- Concatenation – The action of joining two or more words or sections of speech to form a new sentence or phrase. For example in a hospital waiting room you may hear "patient 42, please go to red room 5". In the recording this might have been split into seven separate elements then joined together when played out "patient – forty – two – please go to – red – room – 5".

- Condenser microphone – Most suited to recording studios. On stage you will usually find "dynamic microphones" being used. Condenser microphones have diaphragm plates within which pick up your voice. So for most voiceovers, when shopping for equipment they'll be looking for a large diaphragm, condenser microphone.

- Continuity – The voices that you hear on TV channels with the "that was... and up next is..." information. These are scripted by the voices themselves and are still performed live for larger channels. Satellite channels are mostly pre-recorded then played out.

- Contracting (words) – The act of shortening two words such as "should not" to "shouldn't". It's used either when a script it over-written and you need to save time or when the producer wants to try a more informal/natural sounding read.

- Cool Edit Pro – A popular audio software package now called Adobe Audition.

- Copy – Another word for the script.

D

- De-breath – The process of removing unwelcome breath noises from a recording.

- De-esser – Removes the strong, sharp "SS" sounds from a voice. You can get a live de-esser built into your studio which removes the sound before it reaches your computer or goes down the line to the client. You can also remove the sound in many audio software packages.

- Desk – Usually refers to the mixing desk. So when someone says, "What desk have you got in the studio?", don't say, "IKEA, pine effect."

- Distortion – A corruption of the waveform of a sound wave affecting the frequency or the volume. It will result in less clarity to the recording.

- Double header – Some scripts require two or more voices. A double header is a recording where you will normally be in the same booth or hear the other voice when you're recording. Common examples would be husband and wife scripts or simply just male and female announcers to bring variation to the production.

- Dropout (ISDN) – Heard when an ISDN line temporarily loses connection.

  Permanent drop – It can disconnect completely, requiring you to redial.

  Temporary drop – You may hear silence for a couple of seconds, only if it disconnects then reconnects.

  Glitch – When it loses data for a split second.

- Dry – Used to describe a voice recording which is free from background music and sound effects. Ideally it'll also be free from any audio processing or compression. It's requested by producers who want a completely fresh recording to process themselves or by producers who want to assess studio quality. You should always have a dry recording from your regular setup ready to email a client at short notice if requested.

- Dubbing – Recording a synchronized voice file to overlay a video/film. Usually used when creating multilingual versions of a video.

- Dynamics processing – A type of processing which will boost the lower parts of the sound wave and limit the louder parts. It brings the two volume extremes closer together.

E

- Echo – This shouldn't be confused with reverb. An echo is a distant reflection of a sound which you can clearly comprehend in delay.

- Encoding (telephone audio) – The process of converting a simple uncompressed recording into a specific format using a complex algorithm. It's used in telephone systems where a very small file size is required without the loss of clarity.

- EQ – A filter that can modify the frequencies of a sound wave. You can find a live EQ on a studio desk which will modify the sound before it's recorded, or you can adjust it after recording using the EQ on your audio software.

- Equity – The UK Trade Union representing professional performers and other creative workers from across the spectrum of the entertainment, creative and cultural industries. For more info on Equity please see Question 1.9 "Do I need to join Equity?".

- Exclusivity (agent) – Some agents request exclusivity which means you can only be represented by that agency.

- Exclusivity (recording licence) – A clause in a contract which will restrict you from performing for certain areas of the market or clients which cause a conflict of interest. So if you're the voice of a major mobile phone network, they're likely to want exclusivity to prevent you recording the telephone system for a rival network. Exclusivity will demand a higher fee to cover potential lost work.

F

- Fade – A gradual change in volume either increasing or decreasing.

- Fax and dial – The term was coined by the commercial radio circuit when scripts were faxed and the session was performed immediately after on ISDN. The term is still used but it's more common that scripts are emailed rather than faxed. To be on the fax and dial circuit requires extremely good availability and access to an ISDN studio within a few minutes of being booked.

- Feedback – What you hear when you have an output (headphones/speakers) that can be picked up by your input (microphone). The sound will enter the input, then return through the output and go back into the input again in a continuous delayed loop. It can be caused by having speakers rather than headphones playing audio near a microphone, or by having headphones that are plugged in and left on the desk near your microphone. It can also be caused by having very loud headphones on your head when you record. If it's the latter you might want to see a doctor as your headphones shouldn't need to be that loud!

- Framed (ISDN) – When both ISDN lines connect successfully, the ISDN call is "framed" and audio is travelling happily both ways.

- FTP – File Transfer Protocol. A method of transferring a file from one computer to another. Often you will FTP a file to a web server, making it available to download. Commonly used for files too large to deliver using email.

G

- Gain – The strength of amplification when a signal is sent from one piece of equipment to another. For example you'll have a microphone gain on the mixer which controls how loud the microphone is, as it's sent to your PC or down the ISDN line. Then you'll have a headphone gain to control how loud you hear yourself back.

- Glitch – A term used to describe a small error in a recording such as a skip in the track. They occasionally occur in digital files when finalising a mix, saving the file or uploading/downloading files.

H

- Hard limiting – A simple type of audio compression which caps the volume on a recording to a set level.

- Hz – Hertz is the unit of measurement for the sample rate of a recording. Most recordings will be either 44,100Hz (44.1 kHz) or 48,000Hz (48kHz).

I

- Inflection – The change in tone or pitch in part or all of a word to highlight it. Inflection can go up or down.

- ISDN – The technical name is "Integrated Service Digital Network". It allows you to interact live and in high quality with a producer or client in a remote studio elsewhere. Using an ISDN codec and ISDN lines, they can direct and record you at broadcast quality in their studio, saving travel time and costs.

- ISDN codec – A box that codes and decodes the audio being sent along the line (COde + DECode = CODEC). To prevent your voice sounding like you're on a low quality telephone call, the codec cleverly encodes the audio to make it much smaller in size and easy to send digitally on the ISDN line. The codec in the producer's studio understands this and decodes it to make it sound normal quality.

- IVR – Interactive Voice Response. It's a type of telephone service which allows you to press buttons corresponding to menu options, to achieve a desired path through the telephone system. It's the "press 1 for sales, 2 for returns" kind of script that you might record.

J

- Jobbing voiceover – A voiceover who is hired on a job by job basis, travelling from studio to studio. Generally agency voices who are London based.

K

- Kbps (or KB/sec) – How many "bits" are processed per second (Kilo Bits Per Second), and in an audio file, having a low bitrate will result in poor quality. For MP3 recordings you should deliver at 128 Kbps mono or higher. Don't think that 128 Kbps stereo is the same; it's actually equivalent to just 64 Kbps mono.

L

- Levels – The volumes of different elements on your mixing desk. If a producer says your levels are too high, you probably need to reduce the gain by lowering a fader on your mixing desk channel for your microphone.

- Licence – An agreement with the client allowing them to use your recording on a certain platform, such as television, radio, online. It defines the length/term of the contract, the specific channels if applicable for that platform, territories and also the exposure or number of slots/TVRs for that channel.

- Lipsmacks – Mouth noises that can be the result of a dry mouth.

- Lip synching – When a voiceover watches visuals during the recording session and speaks in time to match the lip movements of those on screen.

M

- Marking up a script – The process of proofing and annotating a script to decide how and where to stress words. Different types of emphasis will be denoted by different symbols to make it clear what type of stress you will apply.

- Mix down – The final version of a production. For example when creating a radio commercial, you might have your voice on one track in the mixer, some music in another track and sound effects in a third track. When you combine all three tracks, the resulting file is called the mix down or bounce down.

- Mixing desk – Used to control different sources of input and output in a studio. It'll allow you to choose what you can hear, what the client can hear and what the computer will record. You might have a small mixing desk in the booth for these basic actions and a more complex mixing desk outside the booth for editing and production, which has additional features.

- Mono – In terms of audio tracks, mono signifies a single channel as opposed to a stereo track which has a left and right channel. For voice recordings you should deliver in mono.

- Monotone – Used to describe a voice which doesn't have variation in pitch and tone, literally meaning a single tone. Another word for this is "flat". It's never normally used in a positive way as it's often describing a voice that you find boring.

- MP3 – In complex terms, this is an MPEG-1 audio layer 3. An MP3 file is a compressed version of an audio file. It does lose a bit of quality in comparison to a WAV or AIFF file but for voice recordings a 128 Kbps mono MP3 is usually fine to work with.

- Muff – The spongy or fluffy black cover for your microphone.

N

- Nasal voice – A voice which reverberates throughout your nose cavities more than your mouth. Please see Question 10.8 "What is a 'nasal voice' and how can I avoid it?".

- Neumann – A well known brand of microphone that's trusted by many voiceovers. More specifically, popular models are the TLM 103, TLM 49, U87 and TLM 193.

- Neutral – A voice that doesn't have a distinguishable accent. Not to be confused with RP (Received Pronunciation).

- Noise gate – Used to eliminate small noises between speech when you're recording. If sound volumes drop below the level that the noise gate is set at, they won't be picked up. This prevents background noises being recorded on the track when you're not speaking.

- Non-union – A term commonly used in the US. A non-union job is a job without any trade union involvement, allowing the client to pay rates lower than the unions recommend. A non-union voice is simply a voice who accepts non-union work.

- Normalisation – A process which applies a constant amplitude change across the full recording to ensure that it doesn't peak over a defined level.

O

- Off mic – When a voice isn't speaking directly into the microphone.

- On-hold (recordings) – Recordings of messages which customers hear when they're placed on hold in a telephone call. They consist of small prompts, normally a paragraph up to around 50 words. A producer will add music and the prompts will be played out periodically.

- Output – A signal that is leaving a piece of equipment rather than entering it.

P

- Pattern (microphone) – Describes the directions that the microphone will pick up sound from. The symbol for a pattern will depict the area it receives sound from, when viewed from above.

- Peaking – If your microphone levels are set too high, you may experience peaking. It's where the signal strength is outside of the acceptable range for your equipment.

- Pencil – A request to hold a time slot for a possible booking.

- Phantom power – Normally supplied by a microphone pre-amp, this is power sent down an XLR lead enabling condenser microphones to work.

- Phone patch – A facility which allows a client to listen in via telephone. It could be hardwired or via your computer.

- Pickup – A re-record of a short section of text. It's usually used when the error is the voice's mistake such as a slur, background noise or mispronunciation, but can sometimes be used to indicate a script change by the client.

- Pitch – The frequency of your voice. For example a child's voice is a higher pitch than an adult's voice and in most cases a male voice is a lower pitch than a female voice. Movie trailers will usually require a low pitch read and upbeat reads will usually require a higher pitch read.

- Platform (licensing) – An outlet where your recording will be used such as cinema, television, radio, internet, telephone marketing etc.

- Plosives – In speech, the action of momentarily stopping the air flow before a consonant. For example when saying the letter "P" you will temporarily close your lips, building pressure and the sound "P" is allowed to burst out when released. Plosives can cause a microphone to pop if spoken directly into it.

- Podcast – A downloadable web-cast rather than a streamed webcast. It's taken from "personal on demand webcast".

- Pop or popping – Certain sounds can generate a forceful breath which will be picked up by the microphone, causing a distortion on the recording. These sounds such as "P", "B" and "Sh" are called plosives. A good pop shield/screen should help solve this problem.

- Pop shield/screen – A perforated shield or screen placed in front of your microphone to prevent popping.

- Post production facility – If productions require additional elements mixed with the voice recording before they're complete, they may be processed in a post production facility. Usually used when mixing audio with visuals either on the fly or retrospectively.

- Projection – The force/penetration of your voice when you speak into the microphone. You would achieve the maximum projection by shouting and the least projection by whispering.

- Proofing a recording – When you listen back through a recording for quality control before delivery. Have you spoken all the correct words? Did you leave in any mistakes? Are the breaths too intrusive?

- Pro Tools – A popular audio software package for recording/editing.

- Pull back – Direction from a producer requesting you to reduce your energy, making your read more natural and less excitable or forced.

R

- Reading to time – Some scripts will require reading within a certain time limit, such as many commercial scripts which are written for a 30 second duration.

- Remote recordings – A session which takes place with the voiceover in a different location to the client or producer. This could be directed over the telephone or recorded down an ISDN line in another studio.

- Retainer – An ongoing payment from a client to a voiceover for services provided on a regular basis. A win/win scenario where the client has better negotiating power and the voiceover gets a regular income. For example the client may pay you £500 a month for up to three 60 minute sessions to update their content.

- Reverb – Audio that's reflected off surrounding surfaces such as walls or the ceiling and bounces back to the source. Although producers may add reverb to their production, a voiceover recording should be completely free of reverb. See "Sound conditioning".

- ROI – A common business term, "Return on Investment" means the income resulting from a particular marketing expense.

- RP – Received Pronunciation. This is a traditional British English accent. Typically "Queen's English" and normally perceived as posh. Not to be confused with the term "Neutral".

S

- Sample – A free custom demo provided to the client as an audition or approval on style before a full recording.

- Sample rate – Measured in hertz, this is the number of audio elements per second in a digital recording. The higher the sample rate, the closer the digital recording is to the original analogue sound. Typically 44,100Hz and 48,000Hz sample rates are used.

- Session – The time allocated for the recording in the studio.

- SFX – Sound effects.

- Sibilance – A strong hissing sound when the letter "S" is spoken.

- Skype – A computer program which allows you to speak over the internet for free to other users with Skype. You can also pay to have an incoming number or make calls to landlines and mobile phones.

- Sound conditioning – The process of softening the inside walls, ceiling and any other exposed surface of a recording booth. Acoustic foam panels and soft furnishings are attached to these surfaces to absorb sound rather than reflect it back into the microphone. This process helps eliminate reverb. Not to be confused with soundproofing.

- Soundproofing – The process of preventing sound entering or leaving a recording booth other than through a microphone. Walls, ceilings and floors will be well insulated with rock wool and various dense material layers. Not to be confused with sound conditioning.

- Source-Connect – Enables high quality audio connections between studios via the internet rather than ISDN. It's a plug-in for certain software packages including Pro Tools.

- Speed read – A very fast read, commonly used to rush through the legal necessities at the end of a radio commercial.

- Spot – This can either mean a single commercial script, or be used to describe a single transmission of that commercial.

- Stereo – A recording with two channels, one for the left audio, one for the right audio. Voice recordings should normally be a single channel (mono).

- Storyboard – Used in productions with visuals. The breakdown of a script into sections, each accompanied by a snapshot of the visuals.

- Synching – Matching an audio track to visuals or to a guide recording. Also see "Lip synching".

T

- Tag – Abbreviation of tagline. A short sentence which ends a commercial script. Sometimes, commercials will have multiple tags, such as, "out next week" and "out now".

- Talkback – A method that allows a producer to chat with a voiceover who is in the soundproof booth.

- TBU – Telephone Balance Unit. See "Phone patch".

- Territory – The countries or areas specified within a licence for use.

- Text-to-speech (TTS) – A system which will take typed text and transform into spoken sentences by concatenating or processing a bank of words which have been recorded by a voiceover.

- Time-stretch – The process of stretching or squeezing a voice recording in order to fit a new time. If a commercial needs to be 30 seconds but the voiceover can't improve upon 31 seconds, then after all breaths have been removed and all else fails, you may resort to stretching the audio to fit the time. It's not advised as it can sound unnatural if you overstretch.

- To picture – A voice recording made whilst viewing the associated visuals.

- TVR – The TVR or television rating is an indication of the exposure a commercial will receive and voice artists can use this to calculate how much to charge for a TV commercial recording. See "Usefee.tv".

- TX – Shorthand for transmission. It really just means the sending of data but it's mostly used in broadcasting. "What's the TX?" of a radio commercial would be "Which stations will it be used on?", and "Don't send that to TX" would indicate that a commercial isn't ready for broadcast.

U

- μ-law – A type of audio file optimised for use on embedded systems, such as a telephone menu. Sometimes written and pronounced as u-law or mu-law.

- Uncompressed (data) – An uncompressed recording is a full size WAV or AIFF file. Requested if the producer wants high quality.

- Undercutting – The act of quoting a lower fee than a competitor (and commonly, lower than the going rate), in an attempt to be awarded a job based on budget rather than voice quality.

- Unprocessed recording – A voice recording which has not been compressed, mixed or tampered with in any way. It's a dry recording.

- Usage – Often refers to an additional payment on top of the session fee which pays for the licence to use the voice recording. Applicable to high profile recordings.

- USB microphone – A microphone with a USB connection rather than a three-pin XLR connection. Typically not considered as good quality as an XLR microphone. They can easily connect to a computer but not to a traditional studio setup.

- Usefee.tv (website) – A website which allows you to calculate a usage fee for television adverts, based on your basic session fee and the TVRs of the campaign.

- USP – Unique selling point. A marketing term that highlights how you stand out from all your competitors.

V

- VOIP – Voice Over Internet Protocol. It's a technology which allows you to make telephone calls using an internet connection, and often a cheaper alternative to traditional copper wire telephone connections, but may not be as reliable.

- Vox – An annual UK conference aimed at voiceovers and producers in the commercial radio market.

W

- Wave/WAV – A high quality format of audio file developed by Microsoft. On PCs, you'll usually use WAVs for high quality storage, and on Macs you'll usually use AIFFs.

- Webcast – A streamed internet broadcast.

- Wild takes (during a session) – The producer might ask you for a few wild takes of a certain line. Traditionally given in batches of three, you'd speak the line in question without reading the content around it.

- Windshield – See "Muff".

- WPM – Words Per Minute. You might see this on a script.

X

- XLR microphone – A microphone with a three-pin XLR connection rather than a USB connection. These are the more traditional studio connections and considered better quality than USB microphones. You would need an adapter to connect an XLR microphone to a standard computer.

Y

- Yousendit.com – One of many file delivery services. Allows you to send large files to clients where email may not be practical.